The Story of Kingston

One of Kingston's most valued possessions is its oldest surviving document—the Charter granted by King John in 1208. It is exquisitely hand-written and bears a fine seal, photographed above, of King John enthroned. The other side of the seal shows the King on horseback.

The Story
of Kingston

JUNE SAMPSON

Dr. E. M. LANCET
Esher, Surrey

© June Sampson, 1972

MADE AND PRINTED IN GREAT BRITAIN BY
THE GARDEN CITY PRESS LIMITED
LETCHWORTH, HERTFORDSHIRE
SG6 1JS

CONTENTS

LIST OF ILLUSTRATIONS

PREFACE

Hardly any books have ever been published on Kingston, and the last narrative history of the town was written as long ago as 1914. This is not because Kingston has no story. Rather its past is so packed with colour and incident that the task of pruning it to fit the confines of the printed page is a daunting—even a presumptuous— one.

I cannot presume to call this "The History of Kingston". For every fact I have set down a hundred equally interesting ones have had to be omitted, and a complete history would require many volumes. A further problem is that everyone has conflicting views on what constitutes local history. Some emphasise the social aspects. Others give preference to topography, or personalities, or historical events. In a book of this size one can only touch briefly on each. However, I have quite deliberately devoted the largest space to Kingston's royal saga, not only because it gives the town a unique historical significance, but also because so little of it has been put into print. Much of the material in this chapter has not, to the best of my belief, been published in any book before.

I have been helped at every stage of my work by the Kingston Borough Librarian and his staff, by the County Archivist and Honorary Borough Archivist; the Assistant Borough Archivist and the staff of the Surrey Record Office; The Market Superintendent and his Deputy; the Secretary of Kingston Hospital and members of Kingston Archaeological Society. I am more grateful to them than I can say for their very considerable assistance—much of it in their own time—and their unfailing interest and encouragement.

JUNE SAMPSON

Royal Echoes

Royal Kingston. The very name distills the echoes of history. Royal vill, Royal Manor, Royal Borough. Such has been the progression from Thames fording place to the thriving centre of commerce and industry that it is today.

Kingston's story is a mirror to the passage and the transience of time. The characters in it are kings and queens, traitors and tyrants, magnates and mountebanks; and the ordinary citizen who has suffered and laughed and cast a sceptic's eye on the events, great and small, that have engulfed him down the centuries.

No town in England has a prouder legacy of the continuity which is our history; few can tell a tale as royal.

This royal story probably began more than 2,000 years ago when the Roman Julius Caesar landed on the Kent coast in 55 B.C. with 600 vessels and 32,000 men. The British Prince Cassivellaunus made heroic attempts to resist the invaders, but to no avail. Caesar and his troops marched steadily through Surrey to a point where the Thames was fordable. The local people had fortified the banks and driven stakes into the river bed but Caesar, forewarned of these precautions, stormed across the water and went on to conquer London.

Historians have argued down the centuries about the exact point where Caesar crossed the Thames. Some have declared it to have been near Chertsey because of the discovery of lead-clad stakes—the Coway Stakes—in the river there. Some say it was Brentford. Others favour Kingston, and the tradition has grown up that it was here that Caesar made the fateful river crossing which was to herald the eventual Roman conquest of Britain. It seems a reasonable assumption. The river was easily fordable here, a fact which was to establish Kingston as a major trading centre, a favoured royal visiting place and the scene of crucial political battles for at least ten centuries. Also many Roman finds have been reported in the past by chroniclers, notably weapons, house foundations and the remains of a mint.

Unfortunately all these decisive finds seem to have disappeared. Nor have there been any recent discoveries to confirm or confound the scepticism of modern archaeologists. They say Kingston's claim to royal Roman importance has never been proved. It has never been disproved either. So the tradition still stands, and the controversy continues.

What is certain, however, is that Kingston was described as "royal" in official documents well over a thousand years ago.

KINGSTON AND THE SAXONS

It was in Saxon times that Kingston entered its golden era of royal associations. The Saxon monarchs probably had a residence here as early as the seventh century, but the oldest existing written document relating to the town is dated 838, and can be seen in the British Museum. It describes the great Ecclesiastical Council organised in Kingston by King Egbert and attended by the Archbishop of Canterbury, twenty-four Bishops and all the leading nobles of the Kingdom of Wessex. This meeting, which set the seal on a compact of mutual co-operation between King and Church, was to have a profound effect on English royal history. Egbert had long planned to strengthen the Throne with such an alliance, and the fact that he chose Kingston for the negotiations indicates its rank and importance at that time.

An even clearer indication of Kingston's standing as the most important of all West Saxon towns, save Winchester, is that after the death of Alfred the Great at least seven of his successors were crowned at Kingston.

Kingston's first Coronation was that of Edward the Elder, son of Alfred the Great, who was crowned here by Archbishop Plegmund in 900. Saxon kings, like rulers centuries before them, were elected by the Witan (or assembly of councillors) then placed on a sacred stone in front of the people.

Edward left a splendid memorial. He succeeded in uniting the divided kingdoms in the land and ended his reign as the first King of all England, and the first to be addressed by the Pope as "the King of the English".

He was succeeded by his son, Athelstan, who was crowned at Kingston in 925. William of Malmesbury, the eleventh-century historian, describes Athelstan as flaxen-haired and slender, and

says he was "crowned at the Royal residence which is called
Kingston". He then quotes an un-named poet, a contemporary of
Athelstan; who describes the scenes in Kingston that day.

> ... the nobles assemble and place the crown, pontiffs pro-
> nounce a curse on faithless men; fire glows among the people
> with more than wonted festivity, and by various signs they
> disclose their deepest feelings ... the great hall resounds with
> tumult, pages scurry to and fro; servers speed on their tasks;
> stomachs are filled with delicacies, minds with song; one makes
> the harp resound, another contends with praises; there sounds
> in unison: "to thee the praise, to thee the glory, O Christ".
> The King drinks in this honour with eager gaze, graciously
> bestowing due courtesy on all.

Athelstan proved himself a great soldier and a firm ruler but,
like all the Wessex kings, he did not have a long life. He was only
in his mid-forties when he died and was succeeded by his
eighteen-year-old brother Edmund.

Edmund was crowned in Kingston by Archbishop Odo in 940.
Five years later he was murdered in his own banqueting hall, and
Kingston was chosen for the Coronation of his brother Edred by
Archbishop Odo in 946. Edred was only in his early thirties when
he died in 955 and Archbishop Odo again travelled to Kingston
to place the crown on the head of Edwy, son of the murdered
Edmund.

Edwy was a headstrong youth of seventeen whose behaviour at
the Coronation feast in Kingston seems highly ill-considered, even
by today's liberal standards.

The *Life of St. Dunstan*, a near-contemporary work written some
time before 1004, describes how a Saxon noblewoman Aethelgifu
and her daughter Elgifu set out to entice Edwy with the aim of
persuading him to marry one of them. The King, it continues,
returned their advances with enthusiasm.

> And when at the time appointed by all the leading men of
> the English he was anointed and consecrated king by popular
> election, on that day after the kingly anointing at the holy
> ceremony, the lustful man suddenly jumped up and left the
> happy banquet and the fitting company of his nobles for the
> aforesaid caresses of loose women. When Archbishop Odo saw
> that the King's wilfulness, especially on the day of his coron-
> ation, displeased all the counsellors sitting around, he said to his
> fellow bishops and other leading men: "Let some of you go, I

pray, to bring back the King so that he may, as is fitting, be a pleasant companion to his followers at the royal banquet."

But one by one, fearing to incur the King's annoyance and the women's complaint, they withdrew themselves and began to refuse.

Finally they chose from them all two whom they knew to be most firm of spirit, namely Abbot Dunstan and Bishop Cynesige (of Lichfield) Dunstan's kinsman, that they should in obedience to the command of all bring the King, willing or unwilling, back to his deserted seat.

When, in accordance with their superiors' orders, they had entered they found the royal crown, which was bound with wondrous metal, gold and silver and gems, and shone with many-coloured lustre, carelessly thrown down on the floor, far from his head, and he himself repeatedly wallowing between the two of them in evil fashion, as if in a vile sty. Then they said: "Our nobles sent us to you to ask you to come as quickly as possible to your proper seat, and not to scorn to be present at the joyful banquet of your chief men." But when he did not wish to rise Dunstan, after first rebuking the folly of the women, replaced the crown, and brought him with him to the royal assembly, though dragged from the women by force.

The King was so incensed by Dunstan's interference that he banished him overseas and married Elgifu, despite the declared disapproval of his Archbishop.

His revenge was short-lived. In 959 there was a rebellion in Mercia and thirteen-year-old Edgar was acclaimed King in opposition to his brother Edwy. Dunstan was immediately recalled from exile, and from then on his rise in the church was swift and unscrupulous. By 959 Edwy was dead and the boy Edgar, a pawn in Dunstan's capable hands, was occupying the throne in his place.

He may have been crowned quietly at Kingston at this time before his splendid Coronation at Bath thirteen years later. Various authorities maintain this view on the grounds that the wording of the service at Bath indicates there had been an earlier ceremony at Kingston.

Edgar's sons, Edward the Martyr and Ethelred II, were both crowned at Kingston by Dunstan, who had become Archbishop. Edward was killed, reputedly at his stepmother's instigation, within three years of his Coronation in 975. His half-brother Ethelred, later nicknamed "The Unready", was only eleven years old when he rode in state to the centre of Kingston in 979 to receive the crown.

The Anglo-Saxon Chronicles record the occasion:

> In this year (979) Ethelred succeeded to the Kingdom, and very quickly after that he was consecrated King at Kingston with much rejoicing by the Councillors of the English people. He was consecrated on Sunday, a fortnight after Easter, and at his consecration were two archbishops and ten Diocesan bishops.

An account of Ethelred's Coronation is preserved in the British Museum, and it is interesting to see how similar is the service to the one used today.

> Two Bishops with the Witan shall lead him (the King) to the Church . . . when the King arrives at the Church he shall prostrate himself before the altar and the Te Deum shall be chaunted. When this is finished the King shall be raised from the ground and, having been chosen by the bishops and people, shall, with a clear voice before God and all the people, promise that he will observe these three rules . . .

Then follows the Coronation oaths, the crowning ceremony, and the giving of the sceptre and rod.

The form of service used at Westminster Abbey for the Coronation of Elizabeth II in 1953 is a legacy of that used at Kingston in the tenth century, and includes prayers, an anthem and the lesson from the old Saxon service.

During Ethelred's reign the Danes ravaged Wessex mercilessly in their bid for absolute power, and Ethelred was forced to flee to Normandy.

The Danish King Sweyn became ruler of England, but died the following year. The English then recalled Ethelred to the throne, and in the bitter fighting that followed Canute, Sweyn's son, was expelled from the country. Within two years Ethelred was dead. His son, Edmund Ironside, was elected King in 1016 and, according to some authorities, was crowned in Kingston.

Immediately after his Coronation Edmund attacked Canute, who had landed in Kent, overcome the south coast and entered the Thames with a vast fleet and army. There was appalling bloodshed and destruction in the Kingston area and many other places before Canute and Edmund finally made a formal agreement to divide the kingdom between them. But Edmund was murdered soon afterwards. Canute was left sole King, and confirmed his title to the throne by marrying Ethelred's widow, Emma.

Thus ended the West Saxon dynasty, and there were no more coronations in Kingston. But a vital part of all the ceremonies still remains in the town. It is the heavy sandstone slab on which the Saxon monarchs are said to have sat to receive their crowns. This unique relic is one of the few Saxon memorials left in England. It stands in a place of honour beside the Guildhall and is the most famous of the few historic treasures that remain in Kingston.

The Mediaeval Period

Kingston was no longer a metropolis, but Canute continued to recognise its royal importance. A document of the period, translated in A. J. Robertson's *Anglo-Saxon Charters*, shows that he was in Kingston to hear the terms of a marriage agreement between Godwine and "the daughter of Brihtric". The bridegroom may have been the same Godwine who, as Earl of Essex, became the most powerful politician in the country.

The same book reveals a great assembly at Kingston when King Canute granted land to Christchurch, Canterbury. The document confirming the grant states that "this was done at Kingston in Surrey on the holy day of Pentecost" and gives a list of witnesses which includes Queen Emma, the Archbishop, three bishops and several nobles.

The next mention of Kingston in a royal connection is in the Domesday Book of 1086, compiled by order of William the Conqueror. Kingston is described as a Royal Manor, which meant that the people there were tenants of the Crown. The book also reveals that King Edward the Confessor and William the Conqueror—a fanatically enthusiastic horseman and hunter—kept part of the royal stud near Kingston.

In 1199 King John ascended the throne, and once again Kingston grew accustomed to seeing a monarch in its midst. For John stayed here many times, and gave the town its earliest existing charter.

This may have won him local popularity, but at national level

John's policies so alienated his people that in 1216 the Barons were finally driven to offer the crown to Louis, eldest son of the King of France. The offer was accepted. Louis landed at Sandwich and, supported by the rebel barons, began to conduct himself as King of England. He soon held half the shires of the country, and might have taken them all had John not died suddenly in 1216.

England was embarrassed. With John safely gone most people wanted only to rally round his nine-year-old son and see him crowned as King Henry III. But how to get rid of the foreign prince whom they themselves had invited to take over the country as King?

After much strife the problem was finally solved in Kingston in 1217. Louis and the Barons came to the town, and were rowed to a small island in the river. Here they thrashed out the terms of the Treaty of Kingston, which saved England from the prospect of complete French control.

The long reign of Henry III brought harassment and destruction to Kingston. Henry was a weak king, whose fifty-six years on the throne were constantly disrupted by the rebellion of his barons and the demands of the Poitevins, who had originally been brought into the country as mercenaries by King John. He was also impoverished. The Exchequer had been depleted by Richard I and John. It was further drained by the greed of the Poitevins, who soon gained a hold on Henry.

It was lack of funds which doubtless caused the King to act with such swift severity when Kingston fell behind with its annual rent to the Crown. In 1226 and again in 1251 the Sheriff was ordered to seize the vill for the King unless arrears were paid immediately. And it was probably to make money rather than through goodwill that in 1256 Henry granted three charters to Kingston, two of them on consecutive days.

Letters Patent of the period show that the King visited Kingston at least a dozen times, doubtless because Kingston was a convenient resting place on royal progresses west.

In 1236 he married Eleanor of Provence, and assigned Kingston to his bride as part of her dower. A fresh swarm of foreign favourites soon followed the Queen to Court, and the anger of the English barons, which had long been simmering against the King, at last boiled up into open resistance.

In 1238, led by the King's brother, Richard of Cornwall, they met together at Kingston while the frightened King took refuge in the Tower. He ultimately yielded, and agreed to the terms of the Kingston conference, but unfortunately the document of the agreement has not survived.

In the following years there was more unrest until, in 1261, Kingston was chosen for a long conference between the two sides. The *Patent Rolls* at this time record the issuing of several safe conduct passes "for the barons coming to Kingston to make peace over the contentions between the King and them, provided they come and stay there without arms".

The assembly at Kingston resulted in an uneasy peace, but in 1263 civil war finally broke out in earnest. For the next three years Kingston, of vital importance because it had the first Thames bridge above London, was occupied by the rebel barons and the town continually burned and looted by their troops. The bewildered townspeople had to suffer the loss of their possessions and the wrecking of their homes through political upheavals—a plight which was to be inflicted on them repeatedly in the centuries to come. Their situation was made worse by floods of such magnitude that entire buildings were swept away (*Calendar of Close Rolls*, 1312).

Initially Henry's eldest son, Prince Edward, attempted to reach a compromise with Simon de Montfort who, as Earl of Leicester, was the most able and influential of the rebels. The Prince agreed to meet Earl Simon at Kingston for a conference. But the talks broke down and, as the prince was about to return to Windsor Castle, he was seized and held prisoner in Kingston. He had to agree to severe terms before he was set free.

Earl Simon then marched on London, reinforced by vast crowds of Londoners who had forced King Henry to retreat from his camp at Southwark.

The following year, with Earl Simon engaged in the Siege of Rochester Castle, Henry set out to re-capture London, marching south from Nottingham. But Earl Simon, warned of his approach, fell back on the capital to oppose him, accompanied by Gilbert de Clare, Earl of Gloucester. Henry's counter-strategy was to by-pass London. He marched to Kingston, and there seized a stronghold said to belong to the Earl of Gloucester, and possibly built to guard Kingston Bridge on land seized by the Earl from the Royal Manor.

Soon afterwards Henry's forces were routed at Lewes, and Earl Simon and the Earl of Gloucester took over the Government. They had only one year of power. In 1265 the Royalists resumed the offensive, led by Prince Edward, and Earl Simon was killed at the Battle of Evesham.

Henry had been dead forty years before Kingston received compensation for its sufferings in the Barons' war. At last, in 1312, Edward II formally decreed that the town could be excused from finding £102 4s. 6d. in rent arrears because they had been caused by the war of his grandfather's time when the town "was on divers occasions robbed and burned" and also because certain buildings had been "wholly carried away" by floods (*Calendar of Close Rolls*, 1312).

The Letters Patent show that Edward I came to Kingston at least four times and signed state papers here. One of his first acts as King was to order the General of his Armies, Pagan de Cadurcis, to prohibit tournaments, jousts or any other armed exercises at Kingston and elsewhere without special licence. The penalty for disobedience was the forfeiture of all lands and property (*Patent Rolls*, February and June 1273 and April 1274).

During the reign of Edward II Kingston once more became embroiled in the smouldering frictions between king and barons. In 1318 Edward's Queen, Isabella, said to be the most beautiful woman in Europe, was refused admission to Leeds Castle in Kent, an insult which Edward used as a pretext for raising a large army against the Constable of the castle, Lord Badlesmere, and other treacherous barons.

In retaliation Roger Mortimer, Queen Isabella's lover, raised men, horses and provisions from his estates in the Welsh Marches and accompanied the armed rebels who swarmed into Kingston demanding the overthrow of the King. Mortimer and his men were met in the town by Lord Badlesmere and other nobles, but almost immediately news reached them there that the King had captured Leeds Castle and imprisoned Lady Badlesmere.

The King's triumph was fleeting. The gathering at Kingston marked the start of an uprising, instigated by the Queen and her lover, which ultimately led to the dethronement and brutal murder of Edward in 1327.

2—TSOK * *

He was succeeded by his fifteen-year-old son, Edward III, who on his accession promptly granted his triumphant mother, Isabella, the annual rent from Kingston for the rest of her life.

It was Edward who changed Kingston's name to Kingston-upon-Thames to distinguish it from another equally important town of the same name which he called Kingston-upon-Hull—more commonly known as Hull.

Edward came to the town several times, including three visits in 1329 and another in 1330. He evidently had a lucky escape from fire while staying in the area in 1353, for the *Calendar of Patent Rolls* records the "appointment of William Waryn of Kingeston, carpenter, and John Sakers whom the King has charged to rebuild at his charges barns and other houses in the manor of the Priory of St. John of Jerusalem in England at Hampton by Kingeston, lately burned by accident by some of the household when the King lodged there, to buy timber and tiles for the work and have them carried to Hampton; and to retain carpenters, sawyers and tilers at work there at the King's wages until the work be finished".

Waryn's work must have been of a high order, for the *Patent Rolls* of 1361 show that the King granted him 3d. a day for the rest of his life.

Edward also had a more personal link with Kingston. He was devoted to his mistress, Alice Perrers, a woman who acquired considerable power over royal politics. By her he had a daughter who married a wealthy Kingston lawyer, Robert Skerne, and lived in a riverside mansion in Kingston called Down Hall. The memorial brasses to this couple are now one of the chief items of interest in Kingston Parish Church.

Edward's death at Richmond in 1377 focused attention on Kingston for, according to the sixteenth-century chronicler Raphael Holinshed, the new King, eleven-year-old Richard II, was staying at Kingston at the time and the people of London sent "certaine aldermen" there to acclaim their new monarch.

In 1392 Hugh Herland, the King's master carpenter, came to live in Bishops Hall, a mansion near Kingston Market which belonged to the Bishops of Winchester. Herland designed the hammerbeam roof of Westminster Hall, commissioned by King Richard and now recognised as the most magnificent work of its kind in the country.

It was fashioned in Farnham, but much of its timber came from Kingston. Herland received a bonus for his work, for the *Patent Rolls* of 1396 decree: "Grant to Master Hugh Herland, the King's chief carpenter, of all the croppings and coppices from the trees and timber bought and provided for the hall within the Palace of Westminster and other the King's works which lie out and remaining over in a wood near Kyngeston-on-Thames."

Richard had ascended the Throne so young that he later had difficulty in breaking the power of the nobles who had ruled during the long years of his minority.

One by one his opponents were removed, and in 1397 Richard laid plans to force through Parliament measures that would give him an almost despotic power. Kingston was the platform of the plan, and on 20 August of the same year Richard ordered Sheriffs throughout England to proclaim that "all lords, knights, esquires and gentlemen who wear the King's livery of the hart [Richard's personal badge was a white hart] all yeomen of the Crown and other yeomen whatsoever who take the King's annuities, wages or yearly fees shall, under pain of imprisonment and forfeiture, be with the King at Kyngeston-upon-Thames at high morn on Saturday the morrow of the Exaltation of Holy Cross next, every man fencibly arrayed and furnished according to his estate and means, to ride with the King to Westminster Palace and there to abide on his service so long as need shall be and order shall be given on his behalf." (*Calendar of Close Rolls*, 1397.)

However, in 1399 Richard was forced to abdicate and Henry IV took the Crown.

Henry's first months on the Throne were hampered by supporters of the usurped King Richard, many of whom had been punished by the loss of land and titles. These nobles embarked on a daring plan to rescue Richard from captivity in Windsor Castle on Twelfth Night, and seize Henry as a prisoner. They arranged to meet at Kingston, using a tournament there as an excuse for taking arms to Windsor. A priest who resembled Richard agreed to impersonate him until he could be rescued.

The conspirators had already gathered at Kingston when news of the plan reached Henry. He fled to London, and the rebels reached Windsor only a few hours after his flight.

Henry's son and heir, Henry V, delighted the townspeople at the outset of his reign in 1413 by nearly halving Kingston's fee farm rent from £50 to £36 per year. He also came to Kingston, and was entertained by Thomas Herland at Bishops Hall (see *Royal Wardrobe Book* in Public Record Office).

Henry VI was only nine months old when he succeeded to the throne in 1422. His reign was disrupted by the prolonged struggle for power between the houses of York and Lancaster, known to history as the Wars of the Roses.

Kingston Bridge played a part in the prelude and the finale to these wars, which were to result in the dethronement of Henry and the placing of the House of York on the Throne.

In 1451 Richard Duke of York tried to persuade Parliament to recognise him as heir to the Crown. He failed, so the following year he raised an army and marched to London from the West Country. The insurgents were prevented from entering the capital, and were forced to cross the Thames at Kingston into the safety of Surrey, and pitch camp on Blackheath.

The ambitious Duke was eventually killed and it was his son who, as Edward IV, succeeded the deposed Henry in 1461.

A glint of royal brilliance was cast on Kingston on 1 October 1467 when Edward IV came with most of the leading nobles of the land to hold a council to agree the terms of his sister Margaret's marriage to Charles, Duke of Burgundy.

The savage conflict of the Wars of the Roses sparked again four years later, and Henry VI was briefly restored to the Throne. But, after bitter fighting, Edward IV regained the crown by defeating the Lancastrians at Barnet and Tewkesbury. Later in the same year Admiral Thomas Neville, better known as the Bastard Falconbridge, made a last attempt to rescue Henry VI from the Tower. He raised a mixed force and mounted a daring attack on London Bridge. But after a brave fight he was forced to retreat. He and his army retired to Kingston, only to find that the bridge had been broken to prevent their crossing. The tramp of their tired feet as they marched away from the town sounded the end forever of the Lancastrian cause.

THE TUDORS AND EARLY STUARTS

Little of Royal note occurred in Kingston while Richard III and Henry VII were on the Throne, but the town became the hub of court activity during the reign of Henry VIII. For in 1525

Cardinal Wolsey gave the King his splendid house at Hampton Court, and many nobles and courtiers were lodged in nearby Kingston.

A more sombre reminder of Royal power came in 1537 when the *Calendar of State Papers Domestic* show that Henry ordered five men to be put to death at Kingston for stealing his hawks and hunting on royal territory.

More drama came to Kingston Bridge during the reign of Henry's daughter, Mary. Sir Thomas Wyatt, violently opposed to the betrothal of the Queen to Philip of Spain, raised an army in a bid to prevent the marriage. Marching with 3,000 men to Southwark he was given enthusiastic support by the people. However, with the guns of the Tower trained on them, they failed to force their way over London Bridge, and instead decided to cross the Thames at Kingston.

The events that followed are described by the sixteenth-century historian Stow:

> On the sixth of February, about 4 of the clocke in the afternoone, he came to Kingston upon Thamis . . . where finding the bridge to be broken, and thirty foote or thereabouts to be taken away, saving the posts that were left standing; and the other side kept by 200 men, he caused 2 pieces of ordnance to be planted against them, whereupon they durst not abide. Then caused he certaine sailers to swim over the Thamis, who loosed the westerne barges, which there had been tied, and so brought them over, by which meanes he passed the water. It was wonder to see what paines he and others tooke, whilst the number of souldiers bayted (ate) in the town; he caused the bridge to be repaired with plankes and beames, the same being tied together with ropes, so as by ten of the clocke in the night it was in such a plight as both his ordnance and companies of men might pass over without perill. And so about 11 of the clocke, Wyat with his band, without resistance, marched towards London, meaning to have been at the court gate before the day of the next morning.

Wyatt's courage and resource led only to defeat. He and many of his followers were convicted of high treason and hanged, drawn and quartered (*Calendar of Patent Rolls*, 1556).

Queen Mary, having married Philip, did not forget her gratitude to Kingston. Because of the considerable losses suffered by the townsmen in defending her against Wyatt, she granted them a third fish weir, free of all rents or other charges, and an additional fair, to be held the day after the Feast of St. Mary Magdalen.

Queen Elizabeth I became a familiar part of Kingston life. She dined here, hunted here and frequently passed through on her way to the Palaces of Hampton Court and Nonsuch.

It was a profitable time for Kingston's ringers, for the bells were rung each time the Queen entered the town. The Churchwardens' Accounts indicate how frequent her visits were. In 1570, for example, they record that "the Queen went in to Berefield" on seven occasions, and the bells were duly rung each time. Berefield, whose location is indicated by the Bearfield Road of today, probably formed part of the Queen's hunting territory.

In 1571 the ringers were paid 6d. for their peal when the Royal Barge was rowed past the Kingston waterside. They received 8d. in 1581 when "Queen's Majestie came from Hampton Court to course" and 5s. when she dined in Kingston in 1597.

The custom of bell-ringing in honour of Royalty finally became so expensive that, as shown in a Court of Assembly Book entry of 1719, it was ordered that the Churchwardens ... "on the King's birthday or any other day of rejoycing relating to the Royall Family shall not expend above the sum of twenty shillings. And they shall not expend or lay out on any other day of publick occasion above the sum of ten shillings (except the fifth day of November)."

It is interesting to see the expenses involved in royal visits. The Chamberlains Accounts, extracts from which are transcribed by Lysons in his *Environs of London*, mention the purchase of gifts for the Queen, including gloves, a scarf and a box. They also list in 1601 the money "paid unto the Queen's Officers their ordinance fees at the time of Her Majestie's coming through the town in her state":

The Serjeants at arms for their fees	20s.
Unto the Trumpeters	20s.
Yeoman Ushers	6s. 8d.
Gentleman ushers	..
footmen	20s.
The Porters	10s.
Lytermen	6s. 8d.
Yeoman of the Botels	6s. 8d.
	Sum £4 10s.

During the 1570s England was stricken by the Plague and, as the Parish Registers poignantly show, Kingston was among the many towns which suffered hardship and death.

As fresh outbreaks of the disease swept the country Kingston made medical history by setting up what was in effect one of the earliest isolation hospitals organised by a local authority. The results were so spectacular that in 1593, when the Plague was still virulent in London, the Queen commissioned a long letter to be sent to the Lord Mayor and Aldermen in which Kingston was cited as an example to be emulated:

> ... for we have seen of late an experience in the towne of Kingstone where the infection did begin very hotlie and in restrayninge and keepinge in those that were infected, the same is ceased. They presentlie upon the fyrste infection, caused an house to be made in the fields dystante from the towne, where the infected might be kept apart and provided for all things convenient for their sustenance and care which, yf so little a town as Kingstone is able to performe, we cannott but thinck that the Cittye of London should, as all other greate citties in Christendom usually do, cause some fitt lodinge to be made in some convenyent place without the cittye where those that are infected might be kept apart ... (*Acts of the Privy Council, 1592–3.*)

Kingston's proximity to Hampton Court Palace, and the fact that many courtiers lodged in the town, encouraged the Queen to keep a specially watchful eye on local health regulations.

In 1578 the Bailiffs were ordered to defer a forthcoming fair and to ban from the town all people coming from infected places.

In 1581, when the weekly markets were attracting great crowds from plague-ravaged London, stern instructions were issued to the Bailiffs. They were ordered to post special guards at all the entrances to the town to enforce the Queen's command to "publicklie prohibite and forbydd all personnes whatsoever, being inhabitantes of the Cittie of London and Westminster or the Liberties near unto them, from henceforth during the tyme of the present infection to resorte within the said towne upon paine of Her Majestie's high displeasure, and to be severlie punished for their contempt to the contrarie ..." (*Acts of the Privy Council, 1581–2.*)

The grim warning to Kingston to "tender Her Majestie's

safetie" was repeated in 1592 with the injunction that "you will answere your negligence to the contrarie upon perille of your lives".

Kingston remained virtually free of the Plague for more than thirty years. Then it returned with great virulence in 1625 and 1636.

Once again the proximity of Hampton Court Palace, and the importance of guarding the sovereign, Charles I, acted as a protective shield for the town. As in the reign of Elizabeth, stern royal instructions were issued curbing the movements of those who had been exposed to infection. In 1625 official documents reported that "the sickness is so violent in London that there is no intercourse of boats from Kingston. At Woodstock, where the Court is, none may go thence to return, nor any come thither, and for contraveners a gibbet is set up at the court gate." (*Calendar of State Papers Domestic*, 1625.)

In 1636, when the disease struck again, Kingston was infected by Londoners who had come to the area to be near the Royal court.

A state document of 19 September decreed that "sheds or hulks are to be built in the fields without Kingston and Hampton and other places within the prohibited distance from Their Majestie's houses and the sick are to be removed unto them." (*Calendar of State Papers Domestic*, 1636.)

Kingston apparently paid little heed to these commands, for only one week later the King's councillors reproved the townspeople:

"There have been frequent commands sent to the bailiffs of Kingston to take care to prevent the spreading of the infection in that town, being situate near His Majesty's house at Hampton Court, notwithstanding which it is found that the houses infected are not kept shut up nor the Red Cross or any other mark set on them, nor any watch set to keep the people therein from going forth or others from visiting them. The persons addressed (Sir John Hippisley and Sir Dudley Carleton) are to call before them the bailiffs of Kingston and examine whose fault this remissness is, and what course is now taken and to take effectual order to hinder the spreading of the contagion; and this they are to see performed, not as Justices of the Peace of the counties adjoining, but as specially appointed by His Majesty for that purpose." (*Calendar of State Papers Domestic*, 1636.)

Pestilence was only one of the tribulations which the local people had to endure during the reign of Charles I. A major source of friction was the King's Saltpetre House in Kingston. Residents in the town, and in neighbouring villages, were perpetually harassed by "Saltpetre Men" who, under Royal Patent, were not only empowered to enter any stable or outhouse they pleased in search of the animal excrement needed to make nitre, but could compel the householder concerned to supply suitable carts to transport it.

In 1625 Francis Vincent, the salpetreman, lodged official complaints against Nicholas Carpenter and Richard Tiler "who being warned to furnish carts to carry liquors from Cheam to His Majesty's saltpetre house at Kingston, being 4 miles, denied the same . . ." (*Calendar of State Papers Domestic*, 1625).

But the loudest outcry was caused—in Kingston as in the rest of the country—by Charles I's chronic shortage of money.

As early as 1625, the first year of his reign, a letter described how "they are in such straits for money at Court as is not to be spoken", and added that the royal troops had been promised payment "as soon as possible" (*Calendar of State Papers Domestic*, 1625).

One result of the King's impoverishment was that for years Kingston was burdened with the expense of lodging and feeding vast numbers of troops. In 1627, after having "for some tyme past entertayned and billetted 140 soljers" (*Acts of the Privy Council*) the townspeople rebelled.

Charles complained through his Privy Council to the Lords Lieutenant of Surrey that soldiers of Sir Peregrine Bartue's Regiment quartered in Kingston "are now putt out of their lodgings by the inhabitantes of the said towne and left destitute by all meanes to furnish themselves with meat and drinck". The letter added that the King "hath commanded us to signifie unto you that it is his express will and pleasure that you, with your deputy lieutenants, doe in personne presently repair unto the towne of Kingestone-upon-Thames and take such effectuall order with the magistrates and inhabitantes of that towne that the soldiers may be provided for that are within that precinct, after the rate of 3s. 6d. the weeke as they have bin hetherto and likewise that care be taken for the billetting of them in such places where they may have lodging and that which is fitting for them . . ." (*Acts of the Privy Council*).

Charles was also driven to revive an old tax known as "ship money", and in 1637 Kingston was charged £81 under this hated levy. The following year it was ordered to join with other towns in commissioning a ship of 400 tons with 160 men to be ready at Portsmouth within four months (*Calendar of State Papers Domestic*).

But the King's most desperate attempt to raise money was his decision to extract enforced loans from the people. Lists were drawn up of the most likely contributors and the sums each could afford. Among the list of Kingston contributors were John Shawe, William Yates and Mark Snelling, each of whom was "requested" to send £10 (British Museum manuscript, *Loans to the King*, 1625).

Nevertheless, Kingston was strongly Royalist in the Civil Wars which were to change England's constitution and ensure the town a coincidental distinction in history as the scene of both the first and last actions of the wars.

THE CIVIL WARS

By 1641 civil conflict between the King and Parliament was inevitable. Parliament had set up magazines of arms and ammunition throughout the country, and the magazine for Surrey and Middlesex was at Kingston. After Charles's desperate and unsuccessful bid to curb the rebels in his Parliament, which sparked the tinder of war, he was forced to retire to Hampton Court. But soon supporters began rallying to his cause at Kingston.

In January 1642 Captain Robert Slyngesbie, one of the only two captains in the Fleet who refused to desert the King, was writing that ". . . there was yesterday a great fear in the City by reason it was reported that Col Lunsford had made proclamation at Kingston for all of the King's party to come to him. If any such thing were, I believe it was but some drunken flourish of those soldiers that followed the King; yet the House has sent order to the Sheriffs to suppress them" (*Calendar of State Papers Domestic*, 1642).

It was more than a drunken flourish. Lunsford had indeed tried to assemble an armed force in Kingston, but he was foiled by the swift intervention of Parliament and arrested on a charge of high treason for "levying war against the King and Parliament". Charged with him was Lord Digby, said by spies to have come to Lunsford at Kingston "in a coach with six horses from Hampton Court".

In his famous *Apologie*, published in January 1642, Digby claimed he went to Kingston merely to deliver a message from the King to the troops, who were growing angry over arrears of pay.

But Parliament was quick to use the Kingston incident to stir up apprehension throughout the country. Leaflets were published describing Lord Digby's design of "levying war at Kingston-on-Thames" and calling for his arrest—though Parliament was well aware that Digby was, in fact, safely overseas.

The campaign worked. People throughout England were soon convinced that their safety depended on supporting Parliament.

From the outset Parliament secured Surrey and its Militia, and a close guard was kept on Kingston because of its magazine, saltpetre works and vital Thames Bridge. Sir Richard Onslow, head of the County forces, posted large detachments of his Militia there and in October 1642 the Earl of Essex, Captain-General of the Parliamentary Army, marched into the town with 3,000 men.

A few days later the King gained an unexpected success at the Battle of Edgehill. Prince Rupert, his cavalry commander, was so heartened by this that he determined to march to London and fight or negotiate at the gates of the capital. The King advanced from Oxford. At Brentford his spearhead troops found themselves threatened by Essex's forces, while the rearguard was exposed to the Militiamen at Kingston.

Prince Rupert decided to attack, and on the night of 11/12 November he routed the Parliamentarians at Brentford. He also managed to blow up the "Kingston Boats"—armed pinnaces which lay in the river at Kingston (Vol. 22, *Surrey Archaeological Collections*).

Hurriedly the Parliamentary troops left Kingston, and the way was clear for the King's men to enter the town to a joyful reception from the residents.

A colourful account of the "liberation" is given in a heavily-biased Parliamentarian pamphlet published at the time under the title *A true declaration of Kingston's Entertainment of the Cavaliers the 13th of Nov.*

A drawbridge had been constructed in the town to strengthen its defences, and the pamphlet describes how it was lowered to let the Royalists in:

> There came first into the towne 600 horsemen and after them 4,000 Welch and Irish Souldiers, who made such spoile that it is impossible that any forraigne enemy had the heart to doe the

like, for in the first place when as they entered the houses they thrust both men, women and children out of doores, and tooke all therein worth the carriage, and what they could not carry they burnt before their faces; unript their beds and made Horse clothes thereof, burnt and spoiled all therein, leaving not so much as an earthern dish to eate their meate upon. There is following his Majestie's army a number of Irish and Welsh women which are of a most barbarous behaviour.

They threaten and put their knives to their wives and children's throates, vowing to murder them if they should not confess or bring forth that which they have or were ever owner of. After this barbarous cruelty in their houses they entered the church, broke downe the Pewes and made fire thereof. They and their horses made Jakes [lavatories] both of the houses and church, and have left the church no better than oxstalls or stables.

The pamphlet adds that the Malignants (the Parliamentarian's name for Royalists) fared no better, even though they had offered to support and feed the Cavaliers.

They were stript to the skinne themselves, all their goodes taken away and their houses worse mortefied than their fellow neighbours.

Yet the pamphleteer has to admit that when Parliamentary forces came two days later to "assist" the people "their hard usage made them forsake them, and they lay great scandals upon Captain Grove which came with the Southwarke Trayned Bands. They were by the inhabitants ill dealt withal, for they would not afford house-roome, nay not so much as food for their money. Captaine Grove, seeing their evil disposition, served them in their right kind, for they would have carried away their goods." Thus the Parliamentary "assistance" was harried out of the town and the Cavaliers "stayed from 1 p.m. on Sunday till Thursday at the same hour, and during this time the town was crueller dealt with than any in his Majestie progress".

The pamphlet says that evidence was given by "those of worth and quality" that when the desperate people of Kingston offered 10s. for a loaf of bread the Royalists refused them any. Instead they stayed until all the food in the town had been eaten. Then they left, taking away all the ammunition in the town "and are since gone to Gilford and about the county where they expect the like prey".

And at their departure they washed the streets with Beere, for there was one Brewer had let run out in the Streets 140 barrels and many quarters of Malt that is spoyled under their feet.

But the bitterest blow to Parliamentary pride was that King Charles won 200 of their troops to his side in Kingston—"scabbed and cowardly fellows fearing lest they should be hanged".

In 1647 there was a lull in hostilities and Sir Thomas Fairfax, commander of Cromwell's magnificent New Model Army, chose Kingston for his headquarters which were housed at The Crane, a fourteenth-century inn near Clattern Bridge. A council of war was held here to discuss peace terms for the kingdom, and the State papers of the period make several references to activities at The Crane, including an assembly of dragoons to escort a consignment of £20,000 to Portsmouth, where it was to be put aboard ship for Weymouth en route to the Parliamentary army in the West.

Fairfax was not comfortable in Kingston. The people made no secret of their Royalist sympathies, and *A Remonstrance from Sir Thomas Fairfax from Kingston-on-Thames*, published in August 1674, states that Parliamentary troops are withdrawing from Kingston because of the proximity of royal troops and because Fairfax finds it expedient to leave a town where he has few friends and where he is "too much pressed and crowded by the great resort of people".

Kingston was weary of playing unwilling host to continuous detachments of soldiers, but had learnt early in the war that protests were useless.

On 22 April 1643 the Bailiffs and inhabitants sent a "humble peticion" to Parliament "that there is due and owinge in the saide Towne, for dyett and other necessaries, for 460 of Colonell Sir Henry Cholmeleyes soldiers, quartered there four weekes fizt from the 13 March last till the 10 April followinge, by warrant from His Excellency, as by billes of particulars may appeare, £289 7s. 2d. And now there are, and for theis 14 daies last past have been billetted by his excellencyes command in this towne about 70 lame and sicke soldiers whose chardge amounts to dayley about 40s." (*KH1/2/1 Borough Archives.*)

The response was discouraging. Within weeks Essex warned the townspeople that all the sick and injured of his regiment were on their way, and he ordered the citizens to "see them provided for and furnished with necessaryes . . . fayle not att your perill." (*KE1/2/2 Borough Archives*). Two days later, on 28 May the Bailiffs sent another "humble peticion" to Parliament, in which they stressed that they had "cheryshed and relieved" some eighty disabled troops for the past two months, and now a further 160 had been sent "to be provided for by us which will be a great charge to us and likely to bringe the infeccion to the Towne". Parliament was asked "that theis new sent soldiers may bee removed to some other place in the countrey who as yett have not been anyway troubled in this kinde." (*KH1/2/3 Borough Archives*).

The reply was brutal. Within six days Essex again sent a train of sick soldiers to Kingston, charging the Bailiffs to nurse them back to health and then "send them safely unto mee into the Armye for the service of the State. Whearof fayle you not as you will answeare the contrary att your perill." (*KE1/2/4 Borough Archives*).

In 1648 Civil War broke out anew and the churchwardens accounts indicate that the King was often in Kingston. In 1648 the ringers were paid 2s. "at several passages of the King through the town" though in 1638, when a zealous Puritan was church-warden, the ringers were paid 6s. 8d. for NOT ringing when the King went through the town.

What is generally described as the last armed engagement of the wars occurred in Kingston in 1648 when the Earl of Holland decided to raise an army in the town to rescue the King from his imprisonment on the Isle of Wight. His main allies in the enterprise were the Duke of Buckingham, General of the King's Horse, and the Duke's handsome young brother, Lord Francis Villiers.

The whole enterprise was a fiasco. The Earl's preparations were totally inadequate, and his plan became such common knowledge that, as he waited in Kingston for officers and men to rally to him, the nobility of London made a pretext of his presence there to visit him in their elegant coaches.

But the Parliamentarians were concerned. Their most impor-tant preoccupation in the June/July period of 1648 was alarm over the gathering strength of the Royalists around Kingston which the Committee of Both Kingdoms, set up by the Parliamentary side to direct the course of the wars, feared could cause the whole of Surrey to fall to the King. On 5 July they wrote to Fairfax, advising him that the Earl and "divers other persons of quality" were at Kingston and would be "very dangerous if not speedily repressed".

The failure of this last Royalist flourish is blamed on the criminal carelessness of the Earl of Holland in *The Decoy*, a pamphlet written immediately after the event by one of the participants.

He relates how they all met together "betweene the two walls neare Kingstone" and, after audaciously seizing horses from the Committee men's houses at Kingston, set off for Reigate. There they were surprised by enemy troops, and in the confusion the Royalist foot soldiers and carriages were sent back to Kingston.

> The enemy had . . . lodged some Dragoons and Musketteers in the brakes and bushes who upon our advance . . . fired their long shot upon our front so thick that there fell down some 12 men in the front and reare, upon the pouring out of which double volley of shot upon us, their whole horse suddenly showed themselves to their best advantage, advancing towards us, upon which some of us cryed out "The Armie, the Armie, we are all betrayed." No stop could be made of our running until we came into Kingston, where we met with our foot who enjoined shame at us and threatened to fire upon us. In Kingston it was often propounded that we should rally, but never effected, yea after the Bridge was stopped by our waggon, the horse drew over in a file. And then for the greater part everyone shifted for himself.

Killed in the battle were Francis Villiers, Col. Thomas Howard, son of the Earl of Berkshire, and twenty officers and soldiers. Another 200 were wounded and 100 taken prisoner. The Parliamentarians also captured nine boats full of pistols and saddles and "good store of pillage" (*copy of letter of 1648 describing the Parliament victory, and preserved in Borough Library Local History Collection*).

The Earl of Holland escaped, but was brought to trial later. His defeat was to have far-reaching effect on many families, for immediately afterwards Parliament confiscated the estates of the King's supporters in Surrey to raise troops of foot and horse in the county.

*   *   *

After the Civil Wars Kingston ceased to be a stage for national events, and all subsequent Royal visits have been of a strictly peaceful nature.

Queen Victoria passed through the town several times and members of the French royal family were married at St. Raphael's Church late in the nineteenth century.

In 1948 King George VI and Queen Elizabeth opened Kingston's new Electricity Power Station in Canbury Gardens and in 1961 Queen Elizabeth II came to Kingston Grammar School to commemorate the 400th anniversary of its foundation by her Tudor predecessor, Queen Elizabeth I.

In 1927 the Mayor of Kingston, Dr. W. E. St. L. Finny, sent a petition to King George V, setting out Kingston's claims to royal status, and asking for confirmation of its title of "The Royal Borough of Kingston-upon-Thames".

The King granted his request, thus confirming Kingston as one of only three boroughs in England privileged to be called Royal, and maintaining a tradition laid down more than ten centuries ago when King Athelstan first described Kingston as a "Royal Town".

1. An early 19th-century drawing of Kingston's riverside. It shows the upstream side of the Bridge, altered in 1912 when work began on doubling the width of the Bridge to accommodate trams.

2. In 1827 a handsome stone bridge replaced the flimsy wooden structure that had made Kingston a strategic point for at least 700 years. The old bridge, once the scene of some of England's most dramatic happenings, remained awhile beside its superior successor, and was sketched by a local resident before it disappeared for ever.

CHAPTER II

"Three Salmon on Blue"

Kingston has enjoyed organised local government for at least 900 years. For the Domesday Book mentions that during the reign of Edward the Confessor, who ruled from 1042 to 1066, the town had Bedels, or locally elected officers.

No further documentary references to Bedels have been discovered, but the name is preserved in Bedelsford, the point where the Hogsmill Stream crosses Brook Street in Kingston, and the name Bedeliscroft occurs in local fourteenth- and fifteenth-century deeds preserved in the Borough Archives.

Domesday also reveals that Kingston was held by the King as a Royal Manor. This meant that the land belonged to the Crown, and the people had to pay rents as tenants of the King. As the King was an absentee landlord, the rents were collected by a Sheriff and Bailiff specially appointed to act as his agents and preside over the Courts of the Manor. There was a Court Baron, which handled land transactions, and a Court Leet, which dealt with petty crime. Serious offences were sent to the Hundred Court (a "Hundred" was the old name given to a county division for administrative and legal purposes. Kingston Hundred included Richmond, Hook, Petersham, Ham and Hatch, Malden, Tolworth and Long Ditton).

Kingston was fortunate to belong to the Crown, for monarchs were invariably short of money, and it was comparatively easy to persuade them to trade many of their manorial rights for hard cash.

Some time during the twelfth century the men of Kingston obtained their freedom and the privilege of holding the town "at farm". This gave them a perpetual lease on the land and the right to collect the town's revenues instead of the King's officials. In exchange they undertook to pay the Crown a substantial fixed annual sum—or "fee farm"—of £28 10s. Once this had been paid they were free to make and administer any further profits.

These privileges were probably granted by Henry II, for in

35

1195 the men of Kingston claimed to have held their town at farm by a charter of "King Henry" which had been "burnt by misfortune", and they applied to King John for a new one.

They had to pay the King 60 marcs. In exchange he granted them in 1200 a charter which increased their annual rent to £40 10s. but gave them authority to elect their own Bailiffs and govern their own town. This charter was the first of some thirty-one to be granted by the Crown up to 1685. The original document has unfortunately been lost for centuries. Otherwise all but two of the town's charters are preserved in the Borough archives.

In 1208 King John, ever in need of more money, pressed a second charter on the town which cost them £100 and raised the annual rent to the then considerable sum of £50. However, it also gave a clearer definition of the rights of the Freemen to govern Kingston without "intermeddling" from the County Sheriff, and to "have and to hold the said town with all its appurtenances . . . and with all the liberties and free customs to which the same town was accustomed". These rights were to last "for ever"—provided they paid their annual rent.

The free tenants of Kingston thus became in effect joint Lords of the Manor, and this charter has always been regarded as the foundation of the Borough's privileges. However, they often had the utmost difficulty in raising the annual £50 for the Crown. In 1226 and again in 1251 the Sheriff was ordered to seize the town if a small balance due to the Exchequer was not forthcoming.

These difficulties made it essential for the townsmen to build up a competent local government administration, able to increase the revenues from the Manor and make "freedom" a viable proposition. Unfortunately, so many of the town's oldest municipal documents have been lost that it is impossible to chart the town's early local government organisation with precision.

In 1441 Henry VI granted the Freeman of Kingston a charter giving them the style and title of "The Bailiffs and Freemen of the town of Kingston-upon-Thames", with the right to meet at the Guildhall to make byelaws for the government of the town and to inflict penalties on those who disobeyed them.

Despite its many privileges the town suffered such poverty and hardship during the fifteenth century that in 1481 Edward IV endeavoured to help by a charter confirming and extending the grants made to the town in previous charters. He also formally created the town a perpetual Corporation with the right to use a common seal.

In this Charter King Edward referred to "the great violent inundations and overflow of the waters lately suffered in Kingston", and added that this and other "burthens" had made the people "injured, deteriorated and so much impoverished that they cannot pay the rent to us and our heirs, and bear the other burthens which lie heavy on the said town".

Until 1835 the main administrative body for Kingston was the Court of Assembly, equivalent to the Borough Council of today. The earliest surviving minutes of this body date from 1680. The loss of the previous minutes, and the fact that there are no town records before the thirteenth century, makes it impossible to say how and when the Court of Assembly originated.

The Freemen so frequently referred to in documents were those who had been elected from the Free Tenants of the Manor to serve on the Court of Assembly. This Court consisted of two Bailiffs, a High Steward, a Recorder, Gownsmen, Peers and Fifteens.

The Bailiffs, whose title was derived from an old French word meaning "administrator", and who were equivalent to the Mayors of today, were elected annually and no Court of Assembly could meet unless they presided.

They were the Lords of the Manor of Kingston, and presided at the Court Baron. They were also judges of the Court of Record and Clerks of the Market. During their year of office, and for twelve months afterwards, they were Justices of the Peace and conducted the Peace and Petty Sessions. They had many other responsibilities, including charge of the jail, the appointment of the jailer and the safe custody of the prisoners. In theory they should have received a reasonable reward in the form of various rents, revenues and tolls awarded to them, but in practice the expenses of holding office outweighed the returns. They were, for example, expected to give at least three public dinners in the year to "neighbouring gentlemen" and members of the Corporation, and to contribute to all public subscriptions. However, a substantial fine could be imposed on anyone who refused to serve as Bailiff.

The office of High Steward probably originated in the sixteenth century, when it was wise to ensure that some important person at court had an interest in the town's welfare. Lord Howard of Effingham seems to have been the first, and is mentioned as High Steward in a book of leases and other grants dated 1584. The appointment was for life, and marked by "a handsome treate" and an annual present of eighteen sugar loaves.

The Recorder was elected by the Court of Assembly and had to be a barrister. He was a Justice of the Peace and presided at the Sessions. He was also Steward of the Court Leet, and was rewarded with an annual fee of £26 5s. and eighteen sugar loaves. One of Kingston's proud distinctions was that it was the only Borough in the country empowered to elect its own High Steward and Recorder.

Gownsmen was the title given to those who had served the office of Bailiff. Fifteens, so-called because of their number, are first mentioned in the sixteenth century. They were all Headboroughs or constables, and liable to serve in that capacity throughout their term of office. Each year they met on the Sunday after Michaelmas and voted out two of their number, who were then known as Peers. The two vacant places were then taken by two men elected from the Free Tenants of the Manor, who were immediately appointed "Ale Conners".

In their oath the Ale Conners were charged to see that "all butchers, bakers, poulterers, fishmongers and all others that set any victual to sale within this town, that the same be sweet and wholesome for man's body; that all brewers who brew for sale any beer or ale doe utter the same in vessels marked of content, according to the statute; and at such rates and prices as are or shall be limited by the Justices of the Peace".

The Ale Conners were also expected to provide a dinner for the whole Court of Assembly on election day, with penalties for those who refused. In 1723 George Malo was fined £10 for "his absolute refusal" to maintain this "antient and laudable custom". His fellow Ale Conner, George Roads, was fined only £5 because he had already given the Headboroughs a breakfast and was "ready and willing to make his entertainment of a dinner if his partner would have joyned with him" (*KB16/11 in Borough Archives*).

The Officers of the Corporation included the Steward of the Court, a largely honorary post held by the Attorney General; the Town Clerk, elected for life to give legal advice and act as clerk to the various courts; two coroners, of whom the Town Clerk was usually one and the junior Bailiff the other; two bridgewardens, elected yearly; two schoolwardens, elected annually to visit and superintend the schools; the Ale Conners and two Chamberlains appointed every year to receive Corporation rents, make payments and keep the accounts. There was also a collector of rents and tolls, two Serjeants at Mace and a Hall Keeper. Other elected officers mentioned in the Bailiffs Minute Books include searchers and sealers of leather and vessels, "hay weygheres", "flesh weyghers", searchers and tasters of bread and supervisors of charitable works.

The entire structure and integrity of Kingston Corporation was endangered during the Commonwealth period when a Roundhead minority managed to seize control of the Borough by unscrupulous and illegal methods.

The leader of the coup was Theophilus Colcock, Bailiff of Kingston from 1653–5 and, in the words of one of his contemporaries, "the most prowd, malicious, insolent, perfidious, turbulent and shameless hipocrite that ever came into any Corporacion".

Documents preserved in the Borough Archives (KB16/7/1–59) indicate that this was an accurate description.

Colcock, with the shadowy backing of his fellow Bailiff Obadiah Wickes, set out to oust all Royalists from the Corporation, to appoint his own friends and relatives to key positions, and to build up a despotic personal power in the Borough.

Early in Colcock's career as a Bailiff in 1653 one of the Headboroughs, John Knolles, was charged with felony after stolen pewter had been found in his shop. He was later proved innocent, but Colcock used the incident as a means of discorporating him, and simply ignored a writ that was issued for his restitution.

Three weeks later another Headborough, Edward Beale, was thrust out of office for refusing to fight against King Charles II at Worcester.

In August 1654 Colcock, supported by Wickes, appointed his prospective son-in-law, Thomas Hancock, as an Attorney at the Court of Record—despite the fact that Hancock was a stranger to Kingston and there was a Corporation rule that there should be no more than four attorneys, each of whom must have served a seven-year apprenticeship in the town.

"I sit not here to be bound up by orders. I sit to make precedents", declared Colcock.

The result, on 17 August 1654, was the most tumultuous Corporation meeting in Kingston's history. John Knolles was said to have "caused a riot" and twenty infuriated Freemen passed a resolution censuring Colcock and Wickes and accusing them of breaking their oaths as Bailiffs in appointing Hancock as Attorney.

Their anger reached boiling point when, two days later, Colcock announced that he wished the office of Town Clerk to be given to John Phelps, Clerk to the illegal court that had condemned Charles I. There were violent protests but Colcock, with his usual cunning, produced a trump card.

Earlier he had obtained a letter from the Lord Protector, Oliver Cromwell, nominating Phelps as Town Clerk. At the height of this meeting Colcock pulled this letter from his pocket and declared "in a terrifying manner" that all who refused to subscribe to Phelps's election would be reported as disloyal to the Lord Protector. Fifteen frightened Freemen then decided to subscribe, but eighteen stood firm, and went off to Whitehall to make personal protests to Cromwell.

While they were away Colcock summoned all his supporters to a secret morning meeting at the Guildhall and discorporated six of his opponents "behind their backes".

This action was so obviously illegal that in April 1655 the ousted members obtained an order from the Upper Bench at Westminster that they should be re-instated.

Colcock and his supporters immediately countered this with a petition to the Lord Protector claiming that *they* were the wronged parties: "In August 1654 a tumultuous assembly met in the Guildhall, and in spite of orders to the contrary sat as a court of common council, censured the bailiffs for their choice of an attorney and discharged them from bearing office. The parties being called to account for their misdemeanours refused an accommodation, on which six of them, three being Headboroughs, were discharged. These, and another discharged for buying stolen goods, have sued out writs of restitution in the Upper Bench . . . we have chosen other Headboroughs but have tendered restitution to the remainder on acknowledgment of their miscarriage, yet they engaging in law suits which will ruin many on both sides" (*Calendar of State Papers Domestic,* 1655).

It is ironical that the matter was referred to Sir Richard Onslow and Col Robert Wood for, only eight months earlier, it was probably Colcock who tried to engineer Wood's dismissal from Parliament. Seven "well-affected persons in Surrey" claimed in a petition to the Government that "Robert Wood of Kingston has been returned Knight of the Shire whom we can prove to be unqualified". They alleged "that he is illegally chosen; is a derider of the people of God; is a profane swearer and of bad life; refused assistance in sending forces to Worcester (to fight the King); is an enemy of His Highness (Cromwell) and the army; opposed the Assessment Commission; refused to pay poor rates; has sided with the cavaliers and in the Earl of Holland's rising engaged never to act against them" (*Calendar of State Papers Domestic,* 1654).

Efforts to bring Colcock and his accomplices to justice continued until after the restoration of the Monarchy under Charles II in 1660. Colcock in the meantime apparently continued to have his arrogant way, illegally appointing and displacing Corporation officers, holding unlawful elections of Bailiffs in his own house and acting illegally over the election of the Earl of Manchester as High Steward.

Finally petitions were sent to King Charles asking for a just settlement of all these abuses. Pending a decision, the King ordered the suspension of the forthcoming municipal elections and ordered the Court of Assembly to elect certain men known to be loyal supporters of the Crown (*Calendar of State Papers Domestic,* 1660).

Even then the irrepressible Colcock was in evidence, having apparently taken possession of the King's orders. These were dated 29 September. On 20 October the then Bailiffs of Kingston were writing angrily to Colcock saying that "if he does not send them by the bearers of the letter the King's mandate and letters, and the Earl of Manchester's letters to the Corporation" they will use force against him.

Colcock blandly replied by return that he had not had time to go to his lodgings, they must excuse him until he could come to Kingston again.

At the Restoration the Church of England resumed its status as the Established Church of the land. But the main strength of the anti-Royalist nonconformists lay in the town corporations, and to deprive them of this the Corporation Act was passed in 1661, decreeing that all Corporation officers must be communicating members of the Church of England and must swear an oath of allegiance to the King.

The Commissioners for the Act came to Kingston in August 1662 to administer the oaths, and list those who refused. The familiar name of Thomas Hancock appears among those who rejected the oaths. He was therefore expelled from his controversial position as one of the town's Attorneys and replaced by James Hargrave.

The name of Obadiah Wickes also appears again. In 1670 he and his wife head the list of those found at an illegal Quaker Sunday gathering in Kingston.

The King's intervention in Kingston's administration, though essential at the time, created a dangerous precedent. Towards the end of his reign Charles attempted to gain more power over the House of Commons by altering the constitution of local Boroughs. Kingston was not then a Parliamentary Borough (it did not become one until 1918) but as Charles already had a foothold in its affairs he decided to make it among the first to be re-modelled according to his new plan.

On 10 January 1685, in a special proclamation, the Bailiffs and Freemen were ordered to surrender to the King all their rights concerning the election of officers. But Charles died on 6 February and the surrender, which was not yet enrolled, was declared void.

However, James II at once renewed the attack on Borough privileges and Kingston Corporation reluctantly made an absolute surrender to him of all their lands and manors and "all franchises, Letters Patents of Incorporation, Powers, Privileges, Libertyes and Immunityes whatsoever."

On 17 July 1685 James issued a warrant for the grant of a new charter to Kingston that "the town shall have . . . a Mayor, High Steward, Recorder, Steward, Town Clerk, Cryer of the Court, 4 Serjeants at Mace, Attorney of the Town Court of Record, 2 High Constables, 2 petty constables, 4 headboroughs. That the Corporation be by the name of Mayor, Aldermen and Burgesses (*Calendar of State Papers Domestic*, 1685).

This Charter was granted on 28 August, and cost its unwilling recipients a substantial fee. It re-organised the Corporation to include twelve Aldermen and sixteen Common Councillors as well as the officers previously mentioned in the Warrant, and declared that all Corporation officers could be removed or replaced by the King. Kingston's earliest surviving Court of Assembly Book shows that James exercised this right with enthusiasm. Between the April and September of 1688 twenty-six aldermen and councillors were removed by the King and replaced by his own nominees. He even discorporated the Recorder, Sir Francis Wythen, and ordered the Corporation to appoint Robert Power instead.

The King's power over Corporation government lasted for three years. Then, as his popularity waned and the threat of invasion by William of Orange grew greater, James was driven to restore the rights of Boroughs by proclamation. In October 1688 Kingston's surrender of its ancient privileges and charters was cancelled and returned to the Recorder, and the previous system of government by Bailiffs and Freemen was restored.

However, James' retraction of his unpopular policies came too late to save his Crown. He was deposed, and in 1689 William and Mary, his son-in-law and daughter, succeeded to the Throne.

The new King became a familiar local figure, for he hunted on the edge of Kingston while staying at Hampton Court. His accession had also saved the Corporation from remaining permanently as a mere Royal pawn. In 1694 the Bailiffs of Kingston sent a Loyal Address to King William (*KB10/4 Borough Archives*), thanking him for his favours and adding: "Now may wee like the Jews of old sitt down every mann under his own Figg tree in peace and safetie reaping the Fruits of his own labours through your Majestie's most gracious protection . . ."

The damage inflicted on the constitution of the Borough, first by Colcock and then by two successive monarchs, evidently drained the vitality from Kingston Corporation. They did indeed "sitt down every man under his own Figg tree", for from the end of the seventeenth century to the reign of Victoria the Court of Assembly sank into apathy and torpor. During that period it was difficult to muster sufficient members to despatch any Corporation business at all, and surviving documents ask despairingly by what means elected officers can be forced to serve.

The magisterial powers of Kingston Corporation extended throughout the four Hundreds of Kingston, Elmbridge, Copthorne and Effingham, so this apathy had a damaging effect on courts serving a very large section of Surrey. By the time the

Commissioner on Municipal Corporations was writing his report on Kingston in 1834 the situation was hopelessly confused.

He found that the boundaries were so complex that no one knew the precise extent of the Corporation's jurisdiction. But his most serious criticism was directed at the quality of the justice meted out in the Corporation courts.

"It has been seen that the town magistrates are the two Bailiffs and their immediate predecessors", he wrote. "It appears from the list of the members of the Corporation that these officers must be frequently chosen from amongst the retail tradesmen of the town. It is said that such persons are too dependent upon the favour of their customers and the goodwill of the townspeople to act with proper energy and impartiality . . . and it appears that the more important business of the town is, when possible, transacted before the County Magistrates."

After more scathing comments on the complacent idleness of the Corporation and the "closed shop" nature of its elections, the Commissioner's report concludes:

> The Corporation as a body is extremely inactive, and with an extensive jurisdiction, numerous officers and a considerable revenue is rather harmless than useful to the town.

When the report was published in 1835 the Corporation was sufficiently roused from its inactivity to send a petition of protest to the House of Lords.

Such a situation would have appalled the Corporations of earlier centuries who fought vigorously to obtain and defend their many privileges.

The story behind King Charles I's charter of 1628 illustrates this.

Towards the end of James I's reign two new dangers arose to challenge Kingston's power and prestige. James had granted the Royal Manor of Richmond to his son, Prince Charles, who became extremely fond of the area. In 1622 the tenants of Richmond petitioned the prince to free them from "subjection to the towne of Kingston".

On two occasions the Bailiffs of Kingston proved to the Prince's Council that they had lawful court jurisdiction over Richmond. But in 1626, after the Prince had become King Charles I, the people of Richmond sent a fresh petition, stressing that Kingston "skymmeth awaie the Creame from his Majestie" because it was able to pocket all the fines imposed by the Court Leet—an argument which the King eventually found irresistible.

Meanwhile the tenants of the Royal Manor of Hampton had announced in 1624 that they intended to apply for the grant of a market. Another market so close by would have robbed Kingston of much of its prosperity, and the Chamberlains Accounts for the year show the various sums spent by the Corporation in preventing the plan, including the gift of "a salmon for Mr. Attorney for his paines".

Both these matters are reflected in the Letters Patent granted by Charles I in 1628. In this Richmond is released from Kingston's court jurisdiction but, as the Bailiffs had undisputably proved their rights, they are compensated by an expansion in the jurisdiction of their Saturday Court of Record and the right of Return of Writ. Also, to prevent any further attempts to poach on Kingston's Market preserves, the documents ordain that there shall be no other market within a seven-mile radius of Kingston.

In 1835, following the unflattering Parliamentary Commission report, Kingston Corporation was remodelled under the Municipal Corporations Act. Bailiffs and Freemen disappeared, and in their places came a Mayor, six aldermen and eighteen councillors, together with a High Steward, Recorder, Town Clerk and other officers. The Corporation was given the new style of "The Mayor, Aldermen and Burgesses of Kingston-upon-Thames" and the Borough was divided into three wards—Town Ward, Ham and Petersham Ward and Surbiton Ward. And, most important of all, the system of election by ratepayers was established.

The Kingston Improvement Act of 1855 increased the Corporation's administrative powers and also extended the Borough to include areas which were formerly parts of the Manors of Norbiton and Canbury. These were made into a fourth ward and two more aldermen and six more councillors added to the Corporation.

Another expansion in administrative powers came in 1900 with the Kingston Corporation Act. This enabled the Town Council to acquire the freehold of the Fair Fields and raise considerable capital for public amenities. These included £15,000 for street widening, £10,000 for an electricity generating station and £6,000 towards a Free Library service.

The spring of 1965 brought the largest reorganisation of local government ever seen in this country. Local administration through-out the Greater London area was re-formed and the former Royal Borough of Kingston-upon-Thames was merged with the Boroughs of Surbiton and Malden and Coombe under the designation of the Royal Borough of Kingston upon Thames (note the removal of hyphens). The Borough is now divided into twenty-four wards, and the Borough Council consists of sixty Councillors elected by the registered voters in the Borough for a term of three years, and ten alderman elected by the Council for either three or six years.

The right to use a Common Seal "to serve for things and business" was officially granted to Kingston by Edward IV in 1481, and a seal thought to date from this period is preserved in the Guildhall. It is a two-inch brass circle, mounted on a wooden handle, and bearing the town's famous Corporate Seal of three salmon swimming on a shield. Around the shield are three lions and the inscription "S. Commun-itatis Ville de Kyngestone Super Tamisiam". It is reproduced on the cover of the Official Guide to the Borough.

Quite apart from the Seal are the Arms of the Borough, first mentioned during the Visitation of the King-of-Arms in 1572.

The Kingston Arms were described as "azure, three salmon naient in pale, argent, finned gules" or, in layman's language, a blue shield bearing three silver salmon, swimming, with red fins.

With the municipal reorganisation of 1965 the Queen issued a Royal Warrant by which the College of Heralds granted Armorial Bearings to the newly-constituted Royal Borough of Kingston upon Thames.

The following interpretation of these Arms is given in the Official Guide to the Borough:

The *Shield* is the ancient coat of arms of the former Royal Borough of Kingston-upon-Thames, recorded in 1572 and 1623. It bears three salmon on blue in reference to the three fisheries mentioned in the Domesday Book.

The *Crest* consists of that of the former Borough of Malden and Coombe, with the addition of that borough's shield hanging from the crown about the stag's neck. The shield has reference to Malden and Coombe's connections with the Crown and Merton College, Oxford, and the stag is a reminder that part of Richmond Park is within this area.

The *Supporters* are those of the former Borough of Surbiton, with its shield hanging from their necks. The elm in the shield recalls the ancient Hundred of Elmbridge and the stags, which link thematically with that in the new crest, are those of the Coutts family.

The whole coat of arms rests on a grassy base edged with waves, symbolising the Royal Borough's situation on the Thames, and preserves virtually intact the heraldry of all the constituent boroughs.

The badge displays the Kingston salmon surrounded by leaves from the Surbiton elm and the Malden and Coombe bay, and surmounted by a Saxon crown in reference to the Royal Borough's title.

CHAPTER III

"*The Beste Market Towne . . .*"

The Royal Manor of Kingston was a highly active rural community long before the Norman conquest of England. It had belonged to the King since Saxon times and the Domesday Book, compiled by order of William the Conqueror in 1086, records that it had a church, five corn mills and three fisheries. It was also engaged in wool production, part of which went to the Queen—"Humfrey the Chamberlain hath one of the villeins belonging to this vill under his direction employed in collecting the Queen's wool".

The land was measured in basic units known as hides and carucates, or ploughlands. A hide differed considerably in size from county to county. A carucate or ploughland was generally reckoned to mean as much land as could be worked by one plough in a year and a day. According to the Domesday Book Kingston, or "Chingestun" as it was called, had thirty-two carucates of arable land, forty acres of meadow and "a wood yielding six swine". The King kept two carucates "in demesne" i.e. for his own use.

There was a section known as the Soke of Chingestun which seems to have been annexed from the original Manor so that part of the royal stud of brood mares could be kept there. The Soke was in the charge of Walter, Governor of Windsor Castle and Warden of the King's Forests in Berkshire, and had an eel fishery, an acre of meadow and a carucate of arable land.

The Abbot of Chertsey also had a small estate at Kingston, granted to him two years before the death of Edward the Confessor. This land, says the Domesday Book, "had previously been held of the King by three homagers who could not remove without the King's precept because they were bedels (locally elected officers) in Chingestun. The arable land amounts to three oxgangs. There are seven oxen, with one border and two acres of meadow."

It is impossible to give an accurate assessment of Kingston's population at this time. Domesday mentions more than a hundred villeins, homagers, bordars and bondmen working the Manor, Soke and Abbot's lands, but takes no account of women and children.

A villein was a peasant who was given land to farm, but in return had to provide labour and services for his Lord of the Manor. A bordar had a cottage and smallholding, but was bound to perform menial tasks for his lord. A bondman was virtually a slave at the bottom rung of the social order.

All of them were completely tied to the land on which they lived. In fact, villein service probably affected about two thirds of the rural population of England. A typical villein would have to plough four acres of the demesne for his Lord at the spring ploughing. He had to provide the oxen for this and for the winter and summer ploughings, and work a minimum of three days a week for his Lord. And at Kingston, if he kept sheep, a substantial part of the wool belonged to the Queen.

In return the Lord of the Manor protected him in numerous ways, and was responsible for his personal safety and the care of his children should they be orphaned.

The life of the average family was therefore one of hard physical labour but little mental stress. It was a simple life, with no chance of travelling or changing jobs. Social pleasures on the rare days of freedom were centred round a variety of jollifications organised by the Church.

It was a pattern of living that was to remain virtually unchanged for centuries, even after Kingston had won its freedom from the Manor system.

Domesday's description, though brief, gives a good indication of local occupations. There must have been a big cereal production to support five mills. Three of them—Hoggs Mill, Middle Mill and Leatherhead Mill—were on the Hogsmill River, and are marked on Rocques's eighteenth-century map of Kingston. Down Hall Mill stood in Water Lane while a fifth mill, judging from references in some of the Borough Archives' sixteenth-century property documents, probably stood about where the Guildhall is now. However, there is no firm evidence that these mills are the ones referred to in Domesday.

The Hogsmill River was known as the Malden River or the Lurteborne until the fifteenth century, and is thought to have got its present name from a miller called Hogg. It is not known exactly when Hoggs Mill disappeared, but in 1845 a miller called Mercer was occupying premises known as "New Mill". This was later acquired by the large milling firm of Marsh, and known as Marsh's Mill until it was swept away to make room for the Corporation Swimming Baths in Grove Road. Marshes also owned Down Hall Mill, a few fragments of which survived until the middle of the present century.

Middle Mill was used in the manufacture of articles from cocoa fibre during the nineteenth century. Leatherhead Mill— sometimes called Chapel or Oil Mill—was the only mill to stay in operation until the twentieth century. Thousands of casks of linseed oil were produced here every year, and the used linseed made into cattle cake. The mill was powered by water, and the noise of the enormous stompers working night and day could be heard for miles around.

Later it became a tallow and candle factory, but during the 1940s the last remains of the Oil Mill buildings disappeared, and the site is now covered by Kingston Corporation's Highways Department. However, the beautiful nineteenth-century Mill House remains on the banks of the river in Villiers Road.

Fishing was a major industry in Domesday Kingston, and for centuries afterwards. The strict religious laws that governed the eating of meat led to an enormous demand for fish and, because of the high cost of sea vessels, the industry flourished in riverside communities. Kingston was especially famous for its salmon, commemorated in the Borough arms to this day, but there was also a brisk demand for pike, eels and even minnows.

The salmon at Kingston were so abundant that in 1781 the apprentices of the town complained at having to eat it more than three days a week.

Most of the villagers kept bees, for honey was the only sweetening agent known to the Anglo-Saxons. The brewing of ale, using malt from local barley, and later of beer, using locally-grown hops, was also important when there was little else for the common folk to drink. In fact, beer and malt production, with its allied trade of inn-keeping, steadily developed into one of Kingston's most famous and prosperous activities. By 1837 the town had thirty-eight rich malthouses, and the famous one in the High Street—a sixteenth-century building that was demolished in

3. An 1840 engraving of the Shrove Tuesday Football which was a riotous annual event in Kingston until it was abolished in 1866. Note the wooden barricades guarding the windows of shops and hotels. Note also the South side of the Parish Church—now much altered in appearance.

4. Kingston Market Place, drawn by Francis Grose in 1770. On the left is the Tudor Town Hall, rebuilt in 1838. In the centre is the 17th-century Oat Market. Under this quaint building, later used as the Town Clerk's office, but demolished in 1796, are the town pump and the stocks, with the pillory hanging alongside. On the right are two ancient inns, the Coach and Horses and The Ship—later renamed The Wheatsheaf, and a favourite haunt of Charles Dickens when he stayed in the area. It is now the NCB Housewarming Centre.

1965 despite a preservation order—was paying one of the largest dues ever recorded in the malting industry right up to the middle of the nineteenth century.

Meanwhile malt was sent downstream to London and, from the seventeenth century, the heavy barges returned to Kingston laden with "seacoal" shipped into London from the north. Thus coal also became an important Kingston commodity and the coal wharves, now disused, can still be seen in the High Street.

One of the town's oldest breweries was that in Brook Street, which was being run by the Rowles family at least as early as 1600. In 1854 the brewery was acquired by Messrs Hodgson and became one of the largest and most important in the country. By 1898 it was producing nearly 1½ million gallons a year, and production increased steadily during the twentieth century. It was eventually taken over by Messrs Courage, but the buildings were destroyed by fire in 1971 while awaiting re-development as shops and offices.

For centuries Kingston was a busy inland port, acting as the main connection to Western Sussex and central Surrey. Many goods were sent from London to Kingston by boat, then completed their journey by road. Other goods were sent by road to Kingston from such places as Dorking and Guildford, and thence by barge to London.

In a charter granted by Charles I in 1628 Kingston is described as "a very ancient and populous town situated on the banks of the celebrated and navigable river Thames . . . from which town, by means of that river, different goods and merchandizes, laden in wherries and boats, are daily transported backwards and forward to our city of London and the adjacent parts".

Timber was an important part of this wharving industry from a very early date, wood from the magnificent Surrey forests being brought to Kingston for shipment to London. In 1259, for instance, large quantities of oak were bought at Kingston for building the royal Palace of Westminster, while much of the wood for the world-famous hammerbeam roof of Westminster Hall came from Kingston in the fourteenth century.

Good supplies of bark, and the proximity of the river, had led to a prosperous tanning industry by the fifteenth century, and in 1850 it was declared that a third of all the leather produced in

Britain was manufactured and dressed in Kingston and elsewhere in Surrey. Kingston's tannery remained near the site of Bishop's Hall, off Thames Street, until it was burnt down in 1963.

Sheep played an important role in Kingston's trading development. Before the rapid growth of the weaving industry in the fourteenth century, most English wool was exported and woven abroad, and the entire wool exports of Surrey passed through Kingston to be taxed before leaving the country.

However, by the beginning of the fourteenth century these mass exports had ceased, and Kingston had established both a wool market and a strong Gild of Woollen Drapers.

Many early documents refer to The Tenterfield, a large stretch of land on the south side of Kingston. This almost certainly got its name from a tenter, an open wooden frame on which weavers spread the woollen cloth they had woven on hand looms in their homes during the early centuries when weaving in England was still only a cottage industry. The tenters were placed in fields which came to be known as tenterfields. Each tenter was the length of a web of cloth, and the weavers had an anxious wait while their cloth hung on tenterhooks until it was shrunk and set and ready for market.

Wool dyeing was practised in Kingston during the sixteenth century, though evidently not of a very high standard. In 1584 three dyers were accused of dyeing articles with logwood at Kingston. James Austen and Richard Rogers were alleged to have dyed a thousand dozen knitted hose with the stuff and Ralph Roodes a "100 pieces of mockadoes". Logwood was imported from America, and many beautiful dye colours could be got from it. But it faded so swiftly that Queen Elizabeth passed an Act abolishing the use of "certain deceitful stuff used in the dyeing of cloth".

Recent excavations have unearthed the fact that pottery making was another early Kingston industry. The Liberate Rolls of Henry III record that between 1264 and 1266 the Bailiffs of Kingston were ordered to send 3,300 wine pitchers to the King's butler at Westminster Palace, and it had been assumed by historians that the pitchers were obtained from a pottery in some neighbouring town. But in recent years the remains of a mediaeval pottery kiln have been found at the back of Nos.

70–72 Eden Street during a dig by Kingston Museum. Part of a clay oven was discovered, together with more than half a ton of pottery, tentatively dated as thirteenth century. It consists mainly of pitchers, in white and buff with a sandy texture, and decorated with rosettes and fir trees.

This pottery works, because of Kingston's efficient river transport, could well have been a major source of supply to London.

Brickmaking, together with pottery, prospered in Kingston right up to the end of the nineteenth century, with Looker's Brickfields and Pottery occupying a large site on Kingston Hill.

The building of Hampton Court by Cardinal Wolsey between 1516 and 1520, and its subsequent conversion to a royal palace in 1530, brought an enormous increase of trade to Kingston. The builders and craftsmen of the town were in constant demand for building and maintenance work; provisions and materials for the palace household were bought in Kingston Market and the inns were frequently filled with courtiers and distinguished visitors who could not find room at the Palace. The State Papers of Henry VIII, to quote examples, refer to the "Ambassadors of Burgundy" and "The Emperor's Ambassador" being lodged in Kingston.

Some Kingston tradesmen depended heavily on the Palace for their livelihood. In 1634, for instance, William Finch complained to the Privy Council of King Charles I that he was "tenant to the King for the sale of tobacco in Kingeston-upon-Thames and Hampton parish, yet receives small benefit except when His Majesty resides at Hampton Court, and then James Lambe, under pretence of being allowed to sell tobacco at Court, disperses his tobacco there to sundry places and persons" (*Calendar of State Papers Domestic*, 1634).

Kingston owed its earliest importance to the fact that it had the first Thames ford, and later the first bridge, above London. There is a theory that the town had a bridge in Roman and Saxon times, but the earliest documentary proof of one is dated 1219 when Matthew de Coventry was appointed Master of the Bridge. It was already endowed with land for its maintenance, and must have been the factor which made Kingston a major trading centre, and its market a venue for customers from many miles away.

It is impossible to say when a market began in the town. The first mention of one is in the Curia Regis Rolls of 1242, describing a dispute as to whether the Bishop of London's men should have been charged tolls on goods they had bought at Kingston Market, but it was obviously a well-established event by then. It also offered a very wide range of merchandise. Letters Patent of 1376, in which Edward III granted Kingston the right to charge tolls on goods passing over the bridge for sale in the town, lists some thirty items including wine, hogs, timber, butter, salmon, salt, arrows, nails and cloth. More valuable privileges were granted in Edward IV's Charter of 1481 which gave Freemen the assize of bread and ale and freedom from the Royal Clerk of the market. Grain is known to have been sold in the market from 1551, and documents in the Borough Archives relating to rents paid to the Corporation between the fifteenth and seventeenth centuries, show that there were wool, cheese, oat and leather markets in Kingston.

In 1603 James I, "desiring the improvement of the town and considering the good and laudable services hitherto often done to and bestowed upon us and our progenitors by the Bailiffs and Freemen", granted the town an extensive Charter which included the right to hold a weekly Saturday cattle market in which "all kinds of animals and live cattle, as well as horses, mares, colts, fat oxen, lean oxen, bullocks, cows, calves, heifers, sheep, lambs, hogs and other living animals of whatsoever kind, nature or species they may or shall be" could be bought and sold there and the Corporation could levy tolls.

This cattle market flourished until the vast building development of the twentieth century swept away all farms from the neighbourhood.

But the greatest royal boost to Kingston Market was Charles I's Charter of 1628.

This granted "that no other market shall from henceforth in future be created anew, or in any manner appointed, or any way held in any place whatsoever within the distance of seven miles from the aforesaid town of Kingston-upon-Thames, either through us, or any one, or any of our heirs or successors".

Such an extensive trading monopoly made it comparatively easy for Kingston to maintain the description given to it by the Tudor historian John Leland in 1535: "Kingeston is the beste market towne of all Southery."

The valuable seven-mile market privilege still applies to the new Borough boundaries as extended by Royal Charter in 1965.

Apart from its market, Kingston also had three annual fairs which brought people flocking to the town in their thousands. The oldest of these was the great Allhallow-tide Fair, which Henry III granted by Charter in 1256. The Fair was to be held "on the morrow of All Souls" (3 November) and for seven days afterwards, but when the new calendar was introduced in 1752, with the "loss" of eleven days, the Fair began on 13 November. By the Victorian era it had dwindled to two days, but Brayley and Britton's *History of Surrey*, compiled in 1850, states that "upwards of twenty thousand sheep, ten thousand head of cattle and one thousand horses have been exposed for sale on a single day in this fair". It was accompanied by a pleasure fair which often lasted the full eight days and was so noisy that the Kingston Improvement Act of 1855 authorised the Corporation to move it from the Market Place and reduce the time allowed. It was moved to the Fairfield and its time cut to three days. Even so the Surrey Comet was describing the event in 1867 as "the concentrated essence of rascality and Black-guardism".

The All-Hallowtide Fair lingered on in steadily decreasing form until the outbreak of World War II, but was finally killed by the urbanisation of the area and the total disappearance of its farms.

Edward III granted the town an eight-day annual fair in Whitsun week and a third fair was granted by Philip and Mary in 1556 as part of their reward to Kingston for resisting the armed rebellion led by Sir Thomas Wyatt against the royal marriage. This Fair was granted for the Feast of St. Mary Magdalen and the day after, and was known as Black Cherry Fair because of the vast quantities of locally-grown fruit sold there. Both fairs were still annual events in Victorian times.

Despite all this trading activity the majority of Kingston people were, like their forebears in the Domesday Book, employed on the land until quite recent times. Crop Returns for 1801 show that 1,546 acres of the parish were under arable cultivation. The main crops were wheat, barley, oats, peas, turnips and rye, in that order, though substantial crops of beans and potatoes were also grown.

Trade Unions did not exist, but all trades and craftsmen, from the richest of the employers to the lowliest of the employed, belonged to a "Gild Merchant" which gave them mutual protection and endeavoured to maintain consistently high standards of craftsmanship and trade methods.

Kingston had such an organisation at a very early date, for in a charter of 1256 Henry III granted that the "men of Kyngeston may have their gild-merchant in their town, as they formerly had it".

There is no record of how this Gild operated before the reign of Elizabeth I but at a Court of Assembly in 1635 a list of rules and regulations was drawn up which was described as virtually the same as one drawn up in 1579.

Under these constitutions it was decreed that the Gild should be divided into four groups known as the Four Companies, and consisting of Butchers (later Victuallers) Shoemakers (later Cordwainers) Woollen Drapers and Mercers. Each Company elected two Wardens annually, and the Town Clerk served as Clerk to the Companies. The members, known as "freemen", had to pay a quarterly subscription to their Company which, by 1834, amounted to 8d. for a married man and 4d. for a bachelor.

For generations the Four Companies had considerable power and influence in the town. No man could carry on a business of any kind in Kingston unless he had first served an apprenticeship there and then been admitted as a freeman to one of the Companies.

Tradesmen who did not meet these qualifications were known as "foreigners" and substantially fined if they attempted to conduct any trade. As late as 1834 three men were fined because, though they were not freemen of Kingston, they had "on two occasions kept open shop". The only exceptions were children and qualified wool combers, who were exempted from such penalties by a statute of George III, and discharged soldiers and sailors, who were protected by a clause in the Mutiny Acts.

However, certain other "foreigners" were allowed to trade in the town if they purchased a "toleration" from the Council, and a number of toleration bonds are preserved in the Borough Archives (*KB19/3/1-47*). For instance, in 1685 John Child was allowed to purchase a bond for £10 because "the trade of a Dyer is very wanting in the towne, there being none other person of that trade".

The Company of Woollendrapers had probably ceased by the eighteenth century. Its dwindling numbers and property at the end of the seventeenth century are noted in the Accounts (*Guide to the Borough Archives*). The remaining three seem to have become profitable pawns of the Corporation. Before being admitted to the freedom of a Company a man had to pay a fee of 6s. 8d. and "the usual stamp of 20s." to the Corporation, while the selling of "tolerations" at between £5 and £30 each was highly lucrative.

By 1834 a Parliamentary Commission was reporting acidly that "the institution of the gild merchant is now a mere source of income to the Corporation", adding that trading itself had become "stationary" in Kingston.

But the coming of the railways was soon to jerk the Corporation from its complacency and change the trading face of Kingston beyond all recognition (See chapter 10).

CHAPTER IV

A Whip for Rogues

Though most Kingston people worked hard and honestly for a living, there was always a substantial number of criminals.

In mediaeval times the duty of helping the poor, though legally the responsibility of the Manor, was generally accepted as being a moral obligation of the Church. Eventually the clergy, the religious houses and the town Gilds were giving alms on such a scale that they actually encouraged people to be irresponsible.

Those claiming alms increased so greatly that ecclesiastical funds could no longer cope with the demand. Beggars began to swarm in the towns and roam the countryside, often degenerating into dangerous rogues and vagabonds.

Mounting violence and crime, and the apathy of the town constables, led to a reign of terror in the Kingston area. The worst outrages seem to have been committed in 1339 in the Manor of Hertingdon Combe, which then formed part of the parish of Kingston, but was later enclosed in Richmond Park by Charles I.

Criminals caused such havoc here that the people were unable to pay their taxes and were forced to petition King Edward III. He ordered his tax collectors to investigate "as the town was lately burned by certain malefactors and all the goods and chattels there were plundered and destroyed, and the inhabitants have for the most part withdrawn" (*Calendar of Close Rolls*, 1339).

The crime wave continued unchecked. Seven years later, in 1346, King Edward condemned the negligence of the Constables stating that "whereas in the counties of Surrey and Sussex divers homicides, robberies and other felonies are perpetrated daily by men called "Roberdsmen', 'Wasturs' and 'Draghlaches', and whereas by the common law of England each should be forthwith arrested by the constables, and if taken within the liberties delivered to the custody of the sheriff, to be kept in prison until the coming of the justices appointed to deliver the gaols, and in the meantime the sheriffs and bailiffs should make inquisitions touching those arrested, nevertheless the constables are negligent in keeping the statute and the said men by day and night run about perpetrating the evils aforesaid".

The King therefore set up a crime squad headed by three Kingston men, Thomas de Purle, John de Codeston and John Scot. Their orders were to arrest and keep in custody "all those of whom there is suspicion of ill" and to cross-examine them closely for evidence. The Sheriff and all the constables, bailiffs and other local government officials of Surrey and Sussex were ordered to help in the campaign (*Calendar of Patent Rolls*, 1346).

There is no further reference to "Roberdsmen, Wasturs and Draghlaches" in the state papers of Edward III, but the situation evidently remained dangerous, for in 1461 Edward IV found it necessary to command the bailiffs of Kingston "to arrest and imprison all evildoers and vagabonds in the town".

Anglo-Saxon society had been marked by widespread violence to property and people, for England then had vast stretches of virgin forest and criminals were difficult to capture.

But in later centuries many villains escaped because of the sheer inefficiency of the police system.

Charles I, in his extensive charter to Kingston in 1628, remarked that he wished the town to be for ever "a town of peace and quiet, to the dread and terror of the bad, and the reward of the good". Local criminals, thriving on the amateur methods used to protect the town, could afford to laugh at such optimism.

From ancient times until late in the eighteenth century every Kingston householder had to take his turn at "watching" in the night from 10 p.m. to 2 a.m. Each Watch consisted of a constable, eight men and the town's Bellman and Beadle. The Bellman kept the rota and warned each man when it was his turn to serve. And, with the help of the Beadle, he had to keep a brightly burning fire and candle in the watchhouse and arrange substitutes for the majority of householders who, dreading the chilly rigours of the night patrol, were only too willing to pay 6d for someone else to watch in their place.

The Bellman was also responsible for keeping a Book of the Watch, listing those who failed either to serve their turn at watching or to pay for a stand-in. This Book was then used as evidence when the reluctant ones were ordered to face the

Magistrates at the Local Sessions. By law men could be jailed for refusing to Watch, but in Kingston they usually escaped with a small fine (*Case on the Custom of Watching in Kingston*, KB16/14).

Watching could be dangerous for untrained amateurs—a fact hinted at in a 1680 entry in the *Court of Assembly Book* ordering that "the muskotts and bullotts lying in the chamber be fitted out and amended for the use of the watchmen on Coombe Park Hill".

This precaution was probably necessary because of the highwaymen who infested the Kingston Hill area. The most famous of them was the eighteenth-century villain Jerry Abershaw, who operated from the Bald-Faced Stag in Kingston Vale. The site of this inn is now occupied by the KLG factory.

Abershaw is also said to have frequented the old Three Compasses in Eden Street—a story borne out by the fact that stagecoach keys were unearthed in the garden there in late Victorian times.

During the eighteenth century crime and immorality in Kingston reached such a level that in 1773 Parliament passed an Act for the Lighting and Watching the Town of Kingston-upon-Thames. This authorised the Corporation to appoint up to fourteen paid watchmen who could be armed at night, build watchhouses and attend to the street lamps. But the Court of Assembly, more fearful of spending money than of a mounting crime rate, took small advantage of the Act, and the number of watchmen was always well below strength.

A Parliamentary Commission on Municipal Corporations, carried out in 1834, made scathing comments on Kingston's watching system. The main weakness was the centuries-old custom whereby the Fifteens—the equivalent of today's Borough Councillors—automatically became "Headboroughs" or constables when they were elected to the Corporation, and could be called upon to serve in that capacity at any time during their year of office. As they were untrained, unpaid and forced to serve whether they wished to or not, their work was so inefficient that in 1823 the High Constables went so far as to present the Headboroughs of Kingston at the Quarter Sessions for neglecting their duties. Ultimately the Headboroughs were only called upon in emergencies, "their station in life" commented the Commission acidly, "unfitting them for the ordinary duties of a constable".

The Commission reported that there were fourteen

Headboroughs and Constables to serve the Hundred while three paid constables and three watchmen constituted the entire "police" force of Kingston town.

"These six are the only effective town officers. There is no system of police" it stated.

In 1835, under the Borough Police Act, the Corporation had to set up a Watch Committee and reorganise its system of watching on the lines of the Metropolitan Police. The nineteenth-century local historian, F. S. Merryweather, describes the officers appointed to guard the night peace of Kingston during this period. They were known as the "old Charleys" and went their rounds with a staff and lantern crying out the hour and condition of the night. One had such an odd voice that no one could understand a word he said. Another had a wooden leg. A third was so old and small that as he shuffled along his lantern dragged the ground. So it is not surprising that the Victorian chronicler W. D. Biden could report that "every vice and every species of immorality appears to have been practised more or less openly in Kingston".

In 1839 an Act was passed empowering the Metropolitan Police to extend its territory to any parish within fifteen miles of Charing Cross. The prospect of having to pay fully-trained police officers so appalled the Corporation that it organised a petition of protest. Fortunately it did not succeed, and in 1840 the Metropolitan Police took over the policing of the Kingston district.

There was no police station, the Corporation having thriftily made the Town Clerk's office serve the purpose after the Borough Police Act of 1836. So in 1864 a new police station was built in London Road, near the junction with Fairfield Road. It remained Kingston's Police HQ until 1968, when new premises were built near the Guildhall.

However, when criminals *were* captured their punishment was ferocious. An entry in the Parish Registers dated 8 September 1572 records:

> This day in this towne was kept the Sessions of gayle Delyverye and her was hangid six persons and seventene taken for roges and vagabonds and whyppid abowte the market place and brent in the ears.

The Chamberlains Accounts for the seventeenth century include such chilling entries as: 1613: a whip for Rogues; 1615: Tow planks to make a pair of Stocks; 1634: a vizard and cap for the whipper; 1636: Stuffe and worke done at the Courthall pillory; 1681: "thirty-three foot of timber to make the gallows" and, in the same year, "to three men for bringing one hundred of Bavins [bundles of brushwood] and fifty fagotts to burne ye woman, 4s."

The Lenten Assize and the Michaelmas Quarter Sessions took place in Kingston. Some calendars of prisoners and proceedings still survive and these, together with the absorbing *Notebook of a Surrey Justice*, compiled by Bostock Fuller between 1600 and 1622, give an idea of the sentences imposed.

Bostock Fuller records that at the Lenten Assize of 1608 William Renfield was sentenced to death for stealing a sheep and a lamb while a man called Burges was burned on the hand for stealing. On other occasions he notes that two men and two women were whipped for stealing ducks and a man who took a goose was put in the town stocks for a night.

The documents of Assizes held at Kingston during the eighteenth and nineteenth centuries are full of hangings and transportations to the Colonies for what would be regarded as comparatively minor offences today.

In 1753, for example, Mary Langsden was hanged for stealing a purse, while in 1779 James Defountain was branded for housebreaking. In 1833 Charles Manmore was sentenced to death at Kingston for stealing a horse while Samuel Rose was transported for seven years for taking a ring.

But the most dramatic sentence of all was reported in the *European Magazine* of 1795:

"Very near thirty years ago a remarkable execution happened no further off than Kingston-upon-Thames in Surrey. One Gregory was hanged for horse stealing, and at the same time no less than eleven of his own sons were hung by his side on the same gallows for repeated crimes of the same nature; and, what is yet more singular, one Colman, with his five sons, were hung on the same gallows at the same moment, in all eighteen in number."

The Surrey Assizes were transferred from Kingston to Guildford in 1884 because of problems concerning the accommodation of judges and other responsibilities. However, they returned to Kingston in 1930, when the County Hall was able to provide vastly improved facilities, and continued to be held in the town until 1971, when the Courts Act replaced both Assizes and Quarter Sessions with a new Crown Court system.

The type of offences dealt with by Kingston's Sessions of the Peace is illustrated by a court list for 1690:

> We present John Blake for keeping of hogs in the Kings Highway from Bishops Hall towards the Markett.
> We present George Dolley of Kingston for a common swearer and cursing and damning the Court and Corporation the 21st April last.

And typical examples from the Bailiffs Minute Book of the eighteenth century:

> 1705: John Turner and John Mitchell, who stole two neckcloths from a hedge, both "listed into her majesties service".
> 1707: Dorothy Terrill set in ye stocks for swearing.
> 1710: Ann Saunders Drunk a Sunday by her owne Confession Ordered to ye stocks for two houres if she can't pay 5s.

The stocks, pillory and whipping post were kept in the Market Place. Public burnings were also carried out there, while hanging usually took place on a stretch of open land at the top of Kingston Hill—an area known as Gallows Hill until it became a fashionable residential district in the late nineteenth and early twentieth centuries.

A special punishment was reserved to cool any hot-tempered women in Kingston. This was the ducking or cucking stool, which consisted of a chair which hung from an axle attached to the end of two long poles. The whole contraption was mounted on three wheels so the victim could be tied to the seat and wheeled publicly through the town to Kingston Bridge, or, in later years, Clattern Bridge.

An early account of a ducking appears in the Parish Registers:

> 1572 August. On Tewsday being the xix day of this monthe of August ... Downing ... wyfe to ... Downing gravemaker of this parysshe she was sett on a new cukking stolle made of a grett hythe and so browght a bowte the markett place to Temes brydge and ther had 111 Duckings over hed and eres becowse she was a common scolde and fyghter [the Christian names have been erased in the Registers].

In 1738 the *Universal Spectator* carried a report of an elderly woman sentenced to a ducking by the Quarter Sessions. This was duly done "and to prove the justice of the Court's sentence upon her, on her return from the waterside she fell upon one of her acquaintances, without provocation, with tongue, tooth and nail and, had not the officers interposed, would have deserved a second punishment even before she was dry from the first".

The use of the ducking stool had ceased by the nineteenth century, but for some time afterwards scolds would be publicly shown up by having the old stool propped up outside their houses.

Charters granted by James I in 1603 and Charles I in 1628 authorised the town to keep its own jail, though in fact there had been a prison in the town well over 400 years earlier. The Assize Rolls of Henry III record that two men escaped from Kingston Prison in 1262, and one fled to sanctuary in the parish church.

In 1264 there was another escape, and the King ordered that William Cotman, keeper of the prison, should be tried to discover whether it took place with or without his knowledge. If it was found that the escape was without Cotman's knowledge, he was to be "delivered from prison after security taken by the Sheriff of Surrey from him for the payment of 10 marcs into the Wardrobe at Easter for the said Escape" (*Calender of Patent Rolls*, 1264).

In 1381 Richard II granted Kingston a shop and eight acres of land to help the town to find its annual rent to the Crown. It is generally thought to be this shop that was later used as the town jail and stockhouse—the store for flax, thread, wood and other items which the parish was obliged to provide "to set the poor on work".

Notes on Corporation property in an old Court of Record Book reveal much about conditions in the jail, referring to manacles and "the yrons remaining in the Stokehouse".

On taking office, jailers of the Stockhouse Prison had to sign a bond undertaking to keep the prisoners securely confined and to preserve the Corporation from expense should any of them escape. Some of these bonds, dating from 1643 to 1781, are preserved in the Borough Archives (*KB19/3/1–47*).

Each is in the sum of £200, and the jailers are all described as Kingston men with occupations ranging from waterman, butcher and shoemaker to that of "gentleman". For the office of jailer was a sought-after one, though it carried little or no wages. The man appointed lived on the premises, renting rooms to the prisoners and selling them food. Those with no money for such luxuries were herded together in one room, and begged from passers-by through the low latticed window. The Stockhouse Jail was mainly occupied by debtors, and when a new Debtors' Prison was built near the Market in 1839 the old Stockhouse became an ale-house known as the Hand and Mace. This was pulled down in 1831, and the Clarence Arms built in its place. This building remained until 1919, when it was acquired by Bentalls, and demolished to make way for the firm's Clarence Street frontage.

An act of 1610 had ordered that Houses of Correction must be built, and that constables should round up rogues, vagrants and other undesirables and send them there. Kingston's House of Correction stood on the site now occupied by the GPO in Brook Street, but was closed in 1852 after the opening of the new County Prison at Wandsworth. The building was then bought as a temporary barracks for the 3rd Surrey Militia and finally became the town's head Post Office after the Militia had built new barracks in Kings Road in 1857.

The Gaol Returns of 1841 praised the House of Correction as "clean, healthy and secure", and remarked that the prisoners performed their work in silence, the men picking oakum and making doormats and clothes pegs and the women sewing, washing and picking oakum.

CHAPTER V

A Charge on the Parish

The actions of unscrupulous criminals and malingerers inevitably increased the sufferings of the genuine poor. As charities were more and more abused, and the number of dishonest vagrants increased, the State was forced to intervene with a series of Acts, each increasing the penalties for vagrancy.

The basis of the system was an Act of 1388, forbidding vagrancy and ordering all "beggers impotent to serve" to remain where they were when the Act was passed. If they could not be maintained there they were to be sent back to their places of birth. Those who disobeyed were whipped for their first offence, had their ears cut off for the second and were hanged for the third.

It was too severe. In 1530 a new Act made a distinction between able-bodied beggars and those incapable of work. The former were whipped. The latter were given licences authorising them to beg within certain defined limits.

Religious houses had always borne much of the burden of supporting the poor, and when they were dissolved under Henry VIII it became essential to draw up new Poor Laws. Each parish was made responsible for its own poor, and clergy and church-wardens were ordered to gather alms from their congregations on Sundays and holidays.

The Parish Registers and Churchwardens Accounts show that in Kingston, as elsewhere, people flocked to the church for money. For example:

> February 1571: Sonday was here two wemen the mother and dowghter owte of Ireland she called Elynor Salve to gather upon the deathe of her howsbande a gentlman slayne amongst the wylde Iryshe being Captaine of Gallyglasses and gathered 18d.
> 1622: "To a poor woman that had her house, husband and child burned 12d", and "to two Scottish merchants that lost their ships, 18d".

But it was the Government of Elizabeth I which, by consolidat-

5. The North side of Kingston Church in 1800. The classical style entrance, in line with the present path from Clarence Street, was removed in 1884 and a new door built further to the right. This doorway is now used as a boiler room, and the main entrance is at the West end. During the 1880's tracery was added to the windows, the present path round the church walls laid, and alterations made to the North and South transepts.

6. Thomas Rowlandson's famous 18th-century picture of Kingston's old bridge and riverside.

ing previous national and regional measures into a single code, laid down the foundations of local Poor Law administration for the next two centuries.

The 1597 Act "for the Suppressing of Rogues, Vagabonds and Sturdy Beggars" ordered that "wandering persons" who refused to work were to be "taken, adjudged and deemed rogues, vagabonds and sturdy beggars" and then "stripped naked from the middle upward and openly whipped until his or her body be bloody; and then sent from parish to parish to his or her last residence, and in default of going there within a time limited to be eftsoons taken and whipped again".

This statute continued for the next 117 years, and the *Bailiffs Minute Book* proves that Kingston took full advantage of it. In 1710, for example, is the entry: "Thomas Doley and Elizabeth his wife and two children Thomas aged 13 and Edward aged 5 years taken begging in ye Town of Kingston . . . adjudged vagrants. The place of their last legall Settlement was in the parish of Inkborough in the County of Worcester. Ordered to be whypt and sent thither."

And in the same year, "Ann Hodsun, a Ragg gatherer, found beggin. To be Whipt".

Where no previous legal settlement could be discovered, the Army provided a convenient outlet. Thus, in 1706, William Robinson and Nehemiah Feare were "adjudged fitt for her Majestie's service" after they had confessed that they did not know their ages, had never been bred to any trade, but had wandered the country looking for work.

The most famous Poor Law Act was that of 1601, under which the churchwardens and two, three or four substantial householders were to be nominated each year as Overseers of the Poor. Their job was to maintain the poor and give them useful work in "habi-tacions", the forerunners of workhouses. The money for this was raised by a levy on every householder.

But still the number of paupers grew, and the Kingston parishioners found it increasingly difficult to support them.

Illegitimate births were a constant burden, The *Bailiffs Minute Book* shows that "lewd idle women" who frequented Kingston's many "houses of ill fame" were put in the House of Correction, while in 1707 "Goodwife Benson ye midwife is strickly forbidd to take any Great bellyed wenshes into her house to deliver them for fear of bringing a charge to ye parish".

Early in the eighteenth century the Kingston Bailiffs decided to take advantage of a law authorising them to force all the paupers in the town to wear badges on their sleeves "in an open and vizible manner". Each badge bore a large scarlet P, for pauper, together with the letter K, for Kingston.

An entry in the *Bailiffs Minute Book* for 1707 reads:

John Saunders and Richard Davison, Overseeres of the Poore, are ordered yt all the poore of this towne have badges on according to the Act of Parliament that receive alms of the towne. Ordered ye next Monday the Bayliffs and justices meet ye overseeres in order to signe ye lists of ye poore and to have the badges put on them.

Paupers who refused to submit to this humiliation had their parish relief stopped. One such rebel was Jeremiah Saunders. He, his wife and their three children had their monthly allowance of 8s. stopped because they were "not badged".

A more practical way of helping the poor had been put forward in 1696 when a petition from Kingston Corporation was read out in the House of Commons stating "that the poor of the said towne daily increase, and are become very burdensome to the inhabitants: that there are large commons belonging to the said towne, clear of timber and of little use; which if improved by sowing flax, hemp etc. would employ their poor, and ease the inhabitants, who are willing to build conveniences for teaching and employing the poor, and their children; which may not only be a comfortable subsistence to themselves, but an advantage to the nation; and praying leave to bring in a bill, empowering them to enclose as much of their commons as they, from time to time, shall find cause to employ for the uses of their poor; and that such enclosures may be exempted from all taxes and tythes".

Sir Richard Onslow was ordered to present a bill to this effect, but for some reason it was never done. A similar suggestion was put before Parliament by Kingston Corporation some years later, but again it was not followed through.

Finally, a vestry meeting was held in 1725 to discuss the problem. The original account of this gathering is preserved in the Archives in a document headed "Scheme for the building of a Workhouse" (*KG3/4/1*).

It states that as "the poor of Kingston are become very numerous and chargeable it would be advantageous to set up a place where they could be "sufficiently maintained and educated and taught to work, read and write, and set to work in order to introduce amongst the poor habitts of virtue, sobriety, obedience and industry and labor, prevent an entail or poverty and idleness and to keep the poor at work and from begging about the streets and pilfering and other vices and idleness" (the underlining is that of the original document).

It was agreed to rent temporarily a house belonging to a Mr. Edward Clive—which old deeds show to have stood near the spot now occupied by Surrey County Hall—at £25 a year, and to raise the necessary funds by levying a poor rate of twelve pence in the pound. The trustees of the enterprise were to be the Bailiffs, Churchwardens, Overseers and "six other persons of ye most substantial inhabitants of Kingston".

They decreed that "all ye males of ye poor (except young children) shall wer one sort of upper coat of a gray color and all ye females shall wer one sort of upper gown of a gray color and all the said poor males and females to wer a badge on their sleeves visibly, ye boys to wer them in their caps".

The rules were strict—"no tipling, smoking tobacco, drinking gin, brandy or buying or selling brandy or strong liquors in the house". Everyone had their appointed tasks, and lazy workers could have no food until their jobs were done. Any fighting, disrespect to the Master or Mistress or other bad behaviour could be punished by three days on bread and water. If the culprit's conduct had not improved by then he was referred to the magistrates and usually sent to the House of Correction.

Children had to have their heads combed "once or twice a day" and be allowed "two hours daily to be instructed to read, write, to cast accounts and to learn them to spinn, knitt or doe some other business or work and not to suffer them in or keep them in idleness".

Paupers had all their goods and chattels confiscated when they entered the Workhouse. These were returned to them intact if they left the Workhouse within a specified period. However, if they were still there after this period had elapsed, the goods were disposed of "for the profit of the house and those therein".

The workhouse system has been severely condemned in modern times, but it is plain that in Kingston, at any rate, its original aim was to treat the poor fairly. The 1725 document decrees that the Workhouse is to be run as a "family", and the Master and Mistress are specially charged to "use all possible care to provide peace and good order in the house and treat the elderly people calmly and tenderly".

A later list of Kingston Workhouse rules, drawn up in 1748 (*document KG3/4/2 in Borough Archives*) shows that the trustees were concerned to see that sick paupers and pregnant women should receive proper care, medical treatment and financial benefits.

The Workhouse was in the charge of a Master who was paid an annual sum with which to maintain the inmates and make a profit for himself. In 1759, for instance, Samuel Plummer was paid £420 a year to provide food, fuel, clothes, medical care and other necessities for the inmates. He also had to pay the rent, provide money for poor apprentices and meet the costs when paupers had to appear before the justices. But he was allowed to set the inmates to work as he thought fit and take the profits. He could also make money for himself by economising on the paupers' food and clothing. The document of 1725 gives a typical week's menus:

	Breakfast	*Dinner*	*Supper*
Sun	bread and beer	beef broth	bread and cheese *or* butter
Mon	beef broth	pease pottage	ditto
Tues	bread and butter or water gruel	rice milk	water gruel
Wed	water gruel	plum dumpling	water gruel
Thurs	water gruel	beef broth	milk pottage
Fri	beef broth	sheeps head	water gruel
Sat	bread and beer	ox's cheek	beef broth

Later in the eighteenth century the Workhouse was in what is reputed to have been the Manor House of Hertingdon Combe. This seventeenth-century house, converted into two and heavily Victorianised, still stands in London Road, opposite its junction with Coombe Road.

As time went on it became increasingly clear that the administration of Poor Law relief had become too onerous to be carried out on a parochial basis. Ratepayers complained with some justification about the burden of the Poor Rates, and pointed out that the paupers were better nourished than many of the honest and industrious poor who had to pay towards their support. In 1835 a committee was formed to inquire into the state of Kingston Workhouse, and their investigations showed the need for reform.

In the following year, under the terms of the Poor Law Amendment Act of 1834, Kingston abolished its old parish Poor Law system and established the Kingston Union. This consisted of three parishes in Middlesex—Hampton, Hampton Wick and Teddington—and ten in Surrey—Kingston, Ham, Hook, Long Ditton, Thames Ditton, Esher, East Molesey, West Molesey, Wimbledon and Malden. These parishes elected twenty-one Guardians, who formed the governing board of the Workhouse and of poor relief throughout the Union.

Just how necessary this reform was is shown by the fact that in 1837 it cost every head of the Kingston population 8s. a year to support the paupers. By 1885 this figure had dropped to 3s. 10d. Further evidence of the success of the Union scheme in Kingston was the Table of Paupers, published in the Surrey Comet on 26 August 1882. This showed that in 1871 there was one pauper to every seventeen of the population. By 1881 the figure had been reduced to one per thirty-eight.

Early documents relating to the Kingston Union have disappeared, but fortunately much of their material is contained in Herbert Broome's booklet *Kingston Union, the Beginning and the End 1836–1930*.

The agenda of Union Workhouse Committee meetings is interesting. For example:

1826: Meat to be baked for Christmas, and the aged, infirm and children will be allowed "plumb pudding".

1838: Married labourers engaged in field work to be paid 1s. 6d. per day and single men 1s. All must work from 6 a.m. to 6 p.m.

1839: Inmates to be allowed a dinner of beef and pudding after the opening of the new workhouse on September 4.

These new premises had been built by the Union in a field in Coombe Lane (now Coombe Road) purchased by the Union in 1837. It cost £10,500 to build, and was known locally as the "Grand Palace". It was an extensive building, in mock Tudor style, with accommodation for 320 paupers. The men were employed in breaking granite, chopping wood and making clothes and shoes for the inmates while the women did domestic work and shirt and bonnet making.

William Sells, in a survey of food and conditions there in 1841, reported that "their pudding would not have been despised by Dr. Kitchener himself". But in 1845 the Medical Officer advised: "I think the health of the children would be much improved by a little meat given daily at dinner. Also that the flour gruel served to the children be made with milk instead of water." The Board adopted his recommendations.

Inmates were given a suit "to wear all day on Sunday" and were allowed to change their stockings once a week.

The worst feature of workhouse life was that paupers of all ages, backgrounds and conditions were herded together. Government legislation gradually improved this situation. Children and old people were transferred to special homes, the sick went to hospitals and the Old Age Pensions Act and Widows, Orphans and Contributory Pensions Acts enabled many people to live in their own homes instead of the workhouse.

The Kingston Union came to an end in 1930 when Poor Law administration throughout the country was transferred from Boards of Guardians to county authorities. Finally, in acts of 1948 and 1966, the central government assumed responsibility for Poor Law policy—by then re-named Public Assistance and, more recently, Social Security.

The treatment of the poor in previous centuries may seem shocking to modern minds. But it must be remembered that in the late seventeenth century more than half the population of England was said to be on the brink of pauperism, and one of the popular songs of the time was "Hang care, the parish is bound to save us!"

By the nineteenth century paupers formed one of the largest economic groups in the country, and in towns like Kingston the poor rate rose so steeply that it caused real hardship to many labouring families. In addition to these high rates Kingston had more than twenty endowed charities which gave various aids to the poor. These charities—fully described in the 1834 Parliamentary Commission Report into Municipal Governments—seem to have been well administered in their earlier years. But during the nineteenth century the management of some of them deteriorated to such an extent that they actually encouraged pauperism, and were denounced by a local vicar as "the curse of Kingston".

The most grossly abused of these charities were *Tiffins*, founded

by the wills of Thomas and John Tiffin in 1638 and 1639 respec-
tively to provide education for "honest poor men's sons"; *Brown's*,
endowed by Elizabeth Brown in 1648 to teach poor children and
put them out as apprentices; *Dollings*, named after John Dolling who,
in 1606, bequeathed £50 so that land could be bought and the rents
given to the poor; the *Countess of Dover's*, named in memory of Mary,
Countess of Dover, who in 1604 gave an annual £5 4s. so that the
Vicar could distribute loaves to the poor every Sunday; *King Charles
I's Charity*, so called because, when the King took the unpopular
step of enclosing Richmond Park, he wanted a piece of land that
had previously been bequeathed to the town for the upkeep of the
bridge. The King bought this land, with the provision that £100 of
the purchase price should be invested for the poor. *Hartopp's
Charity* was founded in 1608 when John Hartopp left £6 from the
rents of his estates to be distributed annually "to not less than
twenty of Kingston's most needy poor". Earlier *Robert Norton* had
left £1 a year in his will of 1599 to buy wood for the poor, while
Edward Belitha's will of 1717 left £400 to buy land and property
whose rents could go to "employing some honest reputable woman,
a legal inhabitant of Kingston, who should be able to read and
work plain work well, to teach twenty poor persons, daughters of
the said town".

Some time before 1624 *Henry Smith* bequeathed £1,000 to
Kingston, instructing that the profits be used to teach poor people
useful trades, to put children out as apprentices and to buy stocks of
goods to "keep the poor in work".

By the 1870s these nine charities were being administered so
dishonestly that Ald Gould—who was Mayor of Kingston in 1853
and again in 1880—made a full report to the Charity
Commissioners.

In an interview with the *Surrey Comet*, published some years
later on 28 July 1900, Gould described the events that led up to his
action:

> "These charities were, by means of petty doles, pauperising a
> number of people instead of accomplishing the good work they
> were intended to do", he said. "On the day of the distribution of
> these doles there was a regular drunken orgy. These charities
> were in the hands of a peculiar set of men, some of whom could
> not even write their own names. These men used to buy up all
> the cottage property in the town, and some of the worst rookeries

in the Borough were known by the names of Rents. Hundreds of people belonging to other parishes used to come into Kingston and live in these wretched tenements in order to take advantage of the gifts which were in the hands of the landlords . . .

"On the day when the doles were distributed the trustees would take possession of the Grand Jury Room to distribute the gifts, which consisted of tickets entitling the holders to jackets, trousers, boots, flannels, bedding and various other things. A number of police were engaged to keep the crowd back, and they used to shut the big doors which then spanned the entrance to the yard of the Assize Courts, opening a small door to let the people in one at a time. Outside was a cursing, fighting, disorderly mob, and the scenes were shocking to witness. It became so bad that on one occasion a woman had her thigh fractured in attempting to get into the yard. As soon as the applicants got the tickets from the trustees, a very large proportion of them sold the tickets, went across the road to the nearest public house and spent the money in drink."

Gould led a vigorous campaign against this system, pointing out that the real object of the charities was to educate the poor.

Of course, the publicans were all dead against me, notably the then landlord of the Griffin, who was one of the trustees.

Finally the Charity Commissioners decreed that all the charities should be amalgamated and used for educational purposes. The result was the revival and re-building of the then struggling Kingston Grammar School and the founding of Tiffin Schools.

"The publicans did their very best—or worst—to defeat the scheme. But the good sense of the townspeople prevailed", declared Ald Gould.

Some years previously, in 1817, the Bailiffs had called a public meeting to discuss the enervating effect of so many charities in such a small town.

The result was an organisation which in its approach might almost have been a product of the twentieth rather than of the nineteenth century. The Kingston Association, set up "to better by every eligible means the conditions and morals of the poor", was in effect a little forerunner of today's National Health and Welfare Services run on a voluntary basis. Initially a survey was carried out to find at first hand the real needs of the poor. This led to a comprehensive social service, including a dispensary, where people could obtain free medical attention; a Clothing and Bedding Society, where the "industrious poor" could get articles at half-price and pay in instalments of threepence a week; public and infants schools, to provide free or heavily subsidised education, and a School of Industry to train young people in useful crafts.

The severe winters of the nineteenth century brought mass unemployment in a town where farming was still a major occupation. In 1861, for instance, the Surrey Comet reported that the doors and passages of the workhouse were crammed with desperate men thrown out of work by the weather, and many families were only saved from starvation by soup deliveries organised by the Mayor and a residents' committee.

By 1885 Kingston had two soup kitchens. One was at St. Paul's School on Kingston Hill, where for 1d. the hungry could get a quart of soup and a pound of bread. The other was at Norbiton Schools, and gave away soup and bread in cold weather.

In 1895 the Thames froze so hard that traffic could cross from one bank to the other, and local traders banded together to help the poor. A rhyme written at the time and printed as a postcard, describes how they gave away 8,000 loaves in one week and adds:

From the Dolphin to the Clarence good sportsmen formed a ring.
Captain Harvey, Phillips, Fricker, George Campbell and young
    King.
The Captain then suggested that five hundred quarts or more
Of soup should be distributed amongst our starving poor.
George Campbell, full of mischief—though a pardonable sin—
When Phillips was not looking threw two legs of mutton in.
When Kingston Corporation took small notice of their poor
A few warm-hearted tradesmen brought the fact home to their
    door.

The old Kingston Union Workhouse, with all its faults and virtues, led to the fine Kingston Hospital that stands in its place today.

Initially the workhouse consisted of workshops, a schoolroom, a hospital, general accommodation and a master's house. In 1843 new wards costing £11,000 were opened for infirm inmates. A further block was built in 1868, and in 1897 the main hospital ward block was opened.

Until 1913 the medical staff consisted of two men—a part-time

Medical Officer and his assistant. Then a second Medical Officer was appointed. World War I began the following year, and the Poor Law hospitals had to cope with the thousands of wounded soldiers who were sent home from service. A section of Kingston's Infirmary, plus a large part of the nearby Norbiton Common Farm were set aside for the troops. Better equipment also had to be provided to deal with the vast increase in surgical work, and when the war ended the authorities realised that what had begun as a wartime emergency measure had become a highly efficient hospital with an important peacetime role.

However, there was strong public prejudice against anything connected with the Poor Law, so Kingston Union Infirmary was re-named Kingston and District Hospital in 1920. The Board of Guardians carried out considerable improvements in accommodation and services, and in 1928 the Duke and Duchess of York officially opened the present nurses home in the hospital grounds. In the following year, when Surrey County Council took over local hospital services, the hospital was separated from the Central Relief Institution, as the Union administration was called, and the hospital was re-named Kingston and County Hospital. By 1936 the Council had prepared plans for the complete rebuilding of the hospital, but war prevented the scheme.

In 1948, with the advent of the National Health Service, a Group Hospital Management Committee was appointed by the South West Metropolitan Regional Hospital Board, and the hospital changed its name for the third time. This time it was re-styled simply "Kingston Hospital".

In 1949 the workhouse accommodation was transferred to the Regional Hospital Board, thus making the whole site available for hospital development. This has included a new Medical Centre, opened by the Minister of Health, Mr. Enoch Powell, in 1962; a new Out Patients Department, opened by Princess Alexandra in 1963 and a new Psychiatric Unit opened in 1966 by Prof. Sir Max Rosenheim.

It is small wonder that the Victorians called their new workhouse the Grand Palace. For the buildings were so well constructed that some of them—extensively modernised—are still in use today. These include the 1843 Infirmary, now known as the Tudor Ward Block; the 1868 development, now called the Extension Block and the 1897 main ward block, which now houses maternity wards, surgical and children's departments and operating theatre suites.

However, they are scheduled to disappear during a massive ten-year redevelopment programme which will provide the hospital with many new facilities.

Kingston's first known hospital existed more than 700 years ago. This was the leper hospital of St. Leonard, whose site and foundation date is unknown, but which was granted Royal Letters of Protection in 1227. Leprosy was rampant in England from the eleventh to the mid-thirteenth centuries, and the "Lazar House"— a chapel and a group of cottages clustering round a green enclosure—was a familiar landmark on the outskirts of most towns. During the fourteenth century many leper hospitals became empty, largely because of the mismanagement and poverty of the charities which maintained them. In any case, most lepers were not anxious for admission because, with hospitals barely able to supply the basic necessities of life, it meant having to endure stringent hospital discipline without any of the former consolatory comforts.

Apparently the lepers of Kingston rebelled in 1315, and showed their independence by not only quitting the hospital, but pulling it down and taking away the materials.

The site, referred to in old documents as "Spitelland", then reverted to the crown, and was granted by various monarchs to their household retainers.

Hospitals in mediaeval times usually meant places where the sick, the poor and the aged could find shelter. They did not, as today, mean centres offering medical treatment. Thus many almshouses were frequently referred to as "hospitals".

Kingston had an almshouse at least as early as 1509, when Cecily Hussie made a will (*Borough Archives KB32/1*) leaving "to the Almshouse for the relief of the poor, a mattress, a pair of sheets and an old white coverlett".

But far better known because it still exists today are Cleaves Almshouses, founded in 1169 for "six poor men and six poor women of honest life and reputation". Money, lands and property for the building and maintenance of this establishment were left by William Cleave, and in 1670 the first residents moved in. Each received £4 a year, free fuel and a new coat or gown, bearing a special badge, every two or three years. Originally the houses were for single people only, but in 1889 married quarters were added.

These almshouses are still in use today. They stand in London Road, near Kingston's famous fourteenth-century Lovekyn Chapel. This building was founded as a chantry chapel by Edward Lovekyn in 1309, but early chroniclers have stated that it was also a "hospitall for the poor". Leland for example, writing between 1535–43, says that attached to the Chapel was "an hospitall, whereyn war a master, two prestes and certen poor men".

The Royal Cambridge Asylum for Soldiers' Widows, whose foundation stone was laid by the Prince Consort in 1825, was in effect an almshouse. It stood in Cambridge Road, near its present junction with Gloucester Road, and provided homes for soldiers' widows who, at that time, received no state benefit of any kind. It was destroyed during the war, and the site is now occupied by large blocks of flats. The only relic of the original fine buildings is a small lodge that still stands at the entrance to the grounds.

Tudor laws had made each parish responsible for its poor so, instead of building hospitals or infirmaries, local governments found it cheaper to send apothecaries or surgeons round the parish to help the sick. However, during the seventeenth century Kingston set up a "pesthouse" for infectious diseases on land known as Marshfield, near the Hogsmill River. Kingston's earliest surviving Court of Assembly Book records that this building was pulled down in 1703, and the proceeds put towards a new poor house in the town.

Apart from the Workhouse Infirmary, the Pesthouse was to be the last organised hospital to be established in the town until 1897 when, to mark Queen Victoria's Diamond Jubilee, the Victoria Hospital was opened opposite the Workhouse in Coombe Lane.

It was maintained entirely by voluntary funds, but was taken over by the State in 1948 as part of the new National Health Service reorganisation. There were bitter protests, many doctors and staff locking themselves in the hospital in a desperate bid to prevent its takeover. They failed, and the Victoria Hospital—whose original buildings are still in use—was merged with Kingston Hospital.

The protesters retaliated by building a New Victoria Hospital in nearby Coombe. It was opened in 1950, and is still in existence, financed by voluntary contributions.

CHAPTER VI

Games and Gaderyngs

Until the nineteenth century the working people of Kingston had virtually no leisure time except on Church festival days. True, no one worked on Sunday. But as it was more or less obligatory to attend church, and as the men in earlier centuries had to take part in shooting practice afterwards, there was little left of the day to call their own.

Those seeking less spiritual pursuits than churchgoing were punished. One of many examples in the *Bailiffs Minute Book* is an entry of 1706: "Thomas Smith paid 5s. for tippleing on the 5th day of May being ye Lord's day in time of Divine Service." And the Churchwardens Accounts of 1625 record "Recd on Sabbath dayes for idle persons being absent from church, 3s. 10d."

Anyone caught working on a Sunday had to face the magistrates, as did Joseph Wyght, a Kingston barber, who appeared at the Sessions of the Peace in 1690 "for trimming of Henry Deale in time of divine service . . . being ye Lord's Day".

After church, throughout the fifteenth and sixteenth centuries, all the able-bodied men of the parish trooped to The Tenterfield where the public archery butts were set up. An Act of 1477 had decreed that every man must be equipped with a bow of his own height and must practice shooting at the town target after Divine Service each Sunday and on holy days throughout the year. This law was reinforced by Henry VII and Elizabeth, and the Borough Archives contain a document of 1565 in which the Bailiffs agree to lease one acre of the "Teynter Field" provided the lessee shall "leave suffycyent waye for ye Archers to go yn and owt to a Rounde stanyng and being in and uppon the seid acre of land above letten at ye east ende thereof nereunto the highway there leadyng from Surpeton to Hogges Myll to pastyme and shoote at ye saide Rounde at all tymes".

Military Service was a universal inconvenience. Kingston, like every other parish, had to provide men for the County Militia. They were usually chosen by lot and had to serve three years or pay £10

for a substitute. Meanwhile all property owners had to contribute
towards the maintenance of soldiers, arms and horses.

When military musters were held the Parish Constables had to
round up the men and escort them to the musters with the parish
arms and armour. This parish armour, which had to be inspected
regularly by the Justices, was valuable. In Kingston it was kept in
the Saxon Chapel of St. Mary, which was used as the parish
storehouse, and it is unfortunate that every item from the collection
seems to have disappeared.

The only reminder that it ever existed occurs in a few
documentary references. Old town accounts, transcribed by the
eighteenth-century historian Lysons, include:

> 1598: To them that wore the town armour two days at 8d. a
> daye, 7d.
> 1603: To James Allison and four other for carrying the
> Armour at the Coronation, 13s. 4d.
> 1603: For armour, £4.

This armour, or harness as it was often called, is also mentioned
in an old Kingston apprenticeship register (*KB11/1/1*, *Borough
Archives*):

> Harness remaynyng in the Store House delyvered to Master
> Carpynter and William Steyns new Baylyffes.
> Fyrst iiii hdd peces
> item iiii swerdes and iiii daggers
> item one corselett
> item iiii hand gonnes and ii touch boxes
> item one pyke.

The Constables also travelled round with press warrants, looking
for men to impress into service. In 1706, for example, the *Bailiffs
Minute Book* records "Edward Beacher, a ladd of 17 years of age,
taken by John Hamond High Constable of Kingston, and John
Banford, Headborough there, having worked 5 yeare on ye river of
Thames adjudged an able-bodied seaman fitt to serve her Majestie
att sea ordered to be sent to ye conductor of ye county to goe on
board her Majestie's Fleet".

It is hardly surprising that when Kingstonians did have a few
hours of freedom they enjoyed themselves with such abandon that
the Bishop and even the King were forced to intervene.

Jousts and other armed sports were a favourite entertainment in mediaeval Kingston, but they became so boisterous that in 1273, and again in 1274, the *Patent Rolls* record that Edward I ordered the cancellation of tournaments in the town.

The churchyard was another favourite sportsground until things got out of hand. In 1393 William of Wykeham, Bishop of Winchester, issued a mandate stating that clergy and lay people used the churchyard for ball games, stone-throwing and other activities, and had caused such damage that "juggling, the performance of loose dances, ballad-singing, the exhibiting of shows and spectacles and the celebration of other games in the churchyard" were to be banned on pain of excommunication.

A famous annual sport in Kingston was Shrove Tuesday football. At 11 a.m. the "Pancake Bell" would ring out and all the apprentices of the town would leave their work to play football in the streets. The game continued until the evening, when everyone joined in feasting and drinking. Eventually the game became so unruly that it was abolished in 1866 despite riots in protest.

The game was said to commemorate a time-honoured tradition that the Danes, in one of their murderous raids on Surrey, were halted at Kingston by the heroic resistance of the townspeople and held until help arrived from London. The Danes were then defeated, their general decapitated, and his head kicked around the town in triumph.

Another old Kingston custom was the cracking of nuts during Divine Service on the Sunday before Michaelmas. The whole congregation joined in, and the noise became so deafening that the practice was stopped late in the eighteenth century. Cracknut Sunday, as it came to be called, was thought to have a connection with the annual election of the Bailiffs and Corporation at Michaelmas and the civic feast that followed.

But the most colourful holiday customs of ancient Kingston were the games referred to in the Churchwardens Accounts as The Kyngham, the Robin Hood, the Lord of Misrule, the May Game and the Hock Game. They probably originated in Saxon or very early feudal times and continued until the sobering advent of the Reformation.

Money collections, or "Gaderynges" were made at these games and handed over to the churchwardens, who then settled all the expenses. Any surplus went towards the maintenance of the church.

The Kyngham was a summer play, featuring a King and Queen of May with their nine dancers and attendants. A stained glass window in Kingston Museum—a twentieth century reproduction of a seventeenth-century design—depicts the Kyngham, and shows the characters and their costumes in detail.

The entertainment possibly originated in Kingston for, though there are references to it in other parishes, it seems to have been performed in Kingston more frequently than anywhere else, not only on a specially appointed annual Kyngham Day, but at other times in the year as well. The Kingston production was apparently so popular that it sometimes went on tour by boat to Thames-side towns from Walton to Richmond.

The Robin Hood Game was held at Kingston each Whitsun and was performed by archers dressed in green who, led by Robin Hood, gave displays of archery. Other leading characters were Maid Marian, Little John, Friar Tuck and a minstrel.

The Lord of Misrule was a prominent festive figure in Tudor England. The King usually appointed a Lord of Misrule to take charge of Christmas festivities in the Royal Household and most of the nobles did the same. The common people also adopted the custom and David Morris, in his *History of England*, describes how every parish had its Lord of Misrule who went about attended by mischievous rustics decked out in gay scarves and ribbons or disguised in animal skins.

The only remaining souvenirs of this custom in Kingston are two receipts of 14s. 6d. in the Churchwardens Account:

1527: Rescd of Lord of Messerville, 14s. 6d.
1530: Recfyd of Lord of Myssruille, 14s. 6d.

In Kingston, as everywhere else in England, the first day of May was regarded as a joyous festival. Bells rang out at dawn, houses were hung with greenery and there were May games in which the people danced around gaily-ribboned Maypoles. A young girl of the town would be elected May Queen and ceremoniously crowned.

The Churchwardens Accounts refer to this May merrymaking:

1516: Paid to the taborer upon May daye, 8d.
1530: Payd for drynke for ye dauncers on Maye Day, 6d.
1569: Item payd to the Ringers on ye ferste Day of Maye.

7. Nineteenth-century Kingston had breweries in Brook Street, Wood Street and High Street. This one in Brook Street was producing nearly $1\frac{1}{2}$ million gallons a year by the end of the 19th century. Owned by Hodgsons, but later acquired by Courage, the brewery remained a familiar landmark until destroyed by fire in 1971. The site was immediately re-developed as shops and offices.

8. Kingston Market Place from Church Street in the 18th century. The inn on the right bears the sign "The Old Queens Head. Horses to let." Today it is the John Quality grocery store. To the left are the Oat Market and old Town Hall.

During the Commonwealth Parliament ordered the destruction of all Maypoles and issued special instructions to churchwardens to see that they were banned from their parishes.

The Churchwardens records are blank for this period, so it is impossible to say if this law was carried out. But the Maypole was certainly revived in the town later, and the custom of dancing around it continued until the mid-nineteenth century when it was carried through the Market Place and put up for May Day in the Apple Market.

Hock Day was the second Tuesday after Easter, when the women of Kingston organised a street "gaderying" in which they captured the men with ropes and made them make a contribution to the church. The men often retaliated with a similar gaderyng, but usually demanded kisses instead of money.

The Churchwardens Accounts show that these Hock Tide gaderyings raised what then represented considerable sums for the church.

The Kyngham and Robin Hood Games were often entered together in the sixteenth-century accounts, and provide interesting information on the cost of food, clothes and labour in Tudor days. For example:

1506–7: Paid for whet and malt and vele and motton and pygges and ges and coks for the Kyngham, 33s.
1507–8: Paid for bakyng the Kyngham brede, 6d. Paid to a laborer for bering home of the gere after the Kyngham was done, 1d.
1508–9: Item paid to John Wonam for a lambe, 16d.
Item paid for III shepe, 5s.
Item paid for half a busshell and half a pecke of flowere, 10d.
Item paid for II women for their labor for II dayes, 5d.
Item paid for turning of the spyttes and for skorying, 7d.
Item paid for the freres (friars) cote, 4d.
Item paid for 2 payre of shone for ye Moreys dauncers, 14d.
1509–10: Item paid for III galonys of mylke, 3d.
Item paid for VI pygges, 2s. 7½d.
Item paid to John a Ham for laboring in ye Kechen, 2d.

The last entry relating to the Kyngham is dated 1524–5, and records that the event raised £7 15s.

"... to Read, Write and Cast Accounts"

Kingston has two proud distinctions in the field of education: it had organised schools at least 700 years ago, and it had the first known public school in England.

The earliest evidence of a school here occurs in 1272 when the name "Magister Gilbert de Southwelle, rector of the Schools of Kingston" appears as the defendant in a law suit. That brief reference indicates that the schools must have been of some quality, for the prefix "Magister" was reserved for the few mediaeval scholars who had completed a full university course, while the title of rector was an honoured one in thirteenth-century educational circles.

In 1364 the Bishop of Winchester—in whose diocese Kingston then lay—wrote to the Canterbury Cathedral Monastery concerning "Hugh of Kingston . . . who presides over the Public School there". This is the earliest reference to a public school ever discovered in this country, and the original letter is still preserved at Canterbury.

Evidently this school, too, was of a high standard. The Bishop's letter records that Hugh was a native of Kingston "where a school has been accustomed to be kept". He had been appointed to "preside over the Public School there", but the almoner at Canterbury was so loath to lose his services that he had kept back some of his possessions in the hope that he would be forced to return. The Bishop demanded the return of these goods, pointing out that the people of Kingston needed a master for "their boys and others coming to the said town". The school was therefore important enough to attract scholars from outside the town and to tempt headmaster Hugh away from a place that was then one of the country's most distinguished centres of learning.

Contemporary documents have been lost, so the location of this school is not known. But it is widely believed to have been in the Lovekyn Chantry Chapel, endowed by John Lovekyn in 1309, and where Queen Elizabeth founded Kingston's famous grammar school in 1561.

There is no direct evidence to prove this. However, Chantry

Chapels usually provided organised education in their neighbour-hoods, and it is significant that the only surviving seals connected with the Lovekyn Chapel, attached to documents of 1368 and 1376, bear the emblem of St. Catherine, the Patron Saint of Scholars. As the Chapel itself was dedicated to St. Mary Magdalene there seems no reason for having such an emblem unless there was a school there. At any rate, the Kingston Endowed Schools governors were sufficiently convinced of the school's pre-Elizabethan existence to change its title officially from the Queen Elizabeth School to Kingston Grammar School in 1904.

The Chantries Act of 1547 abolished all chantry chapels whose *original* statutes did not specify the maintenance of a school. The Lovekyn Chapel came into this category, so it was closed and all its endowments seized for King Edward VI.

After the accession of Mary in 1553, and Elizabeth in 1558, many towns petitioned for the re-establishment of schools lost through the Chantries Act. Thus, in Letters Patent issued by Elizabeth in 1561, she mentions "that at the humble petition of our beloved subjects . . . of our town of Kingeston-upon-Thames . . . for a grammar school within the aforesaid parish of Kingeston to be erected and established for the training and instruction of boys and youths . . . we will, grant and ordain for us and our heirs that henceforth there be and shall be a grammar school to ensure for ever in the said towne . . . which shall be called the Free Grammar School of Queen Elizabeth, for the education, training and instruction of boys and youths in grammar".

Three years later the Queen presented the school with more than a hundred acres of land and some thirty properties so the Master's salary could be increased and the school better maintained.

The school has survived, with varying degrees of success, until the present time. Rules drawn up in 1671 by the Bailiffs of Kingston, who were the governors of the school, stipulated that "children borne in the Towne shall be taught freely, and others that are ye Children of the Inhabitants of the Towne shall pay one shilling a piece by the Quarter" and that "children thus admitted shall be carefully kept to their learning all the dayes of the weeke (except Sundayes, holydayes and the three Faire dayes) from seaven of the clock in the morning till eleaven and from one of the clock in ye afternoon till five, unlesse in the short dayes of winter when the Schoole time shall begin and end with the light by which they may well see to read".

But in 1732 the Rev Richard Wooddeson was appointed Master, and raised the school to such a high standard that rich men's sons came flocking there to the virtual exclusion of the poor. When Wooddeson left the school declined, and was soon deep in debt, partly because of the apathy of the Bailiffs as governors, and partly because a large part of the lands granted to the school by Elizabeth were misappropriated by the Corporation during the sixteenth and seventeenth centuries. By the nineteenth century the school had sunk so low that in 1874 Queen Victoria gave her assent to a scheme by the Endowed Schools Commissioners to take charge of the school and of the Tiffin foundation, an educational charity founded by the Tiffin brothers in the seventeenth century. It was agreed that the endowments of the two organisations should be combined, then divided between them. At the same time many old Kingston charities were absorbed into the new scheme, and their proceeds devoted to education (see Chapter V).

The scheme resulted in the construction of new Grammar School buildings opposite the original chapel premises in London Road and the establishment of a lower mixed school named Tiffin School. However, the bulk of the endowment funds was lavished on Tiffins at the expense of the Grammar School. In 1880 Tiffins Boys School opened on the Fairfield and in 1890 handsome new buildings were provided for Tiffin Girls School. Eventually the Grammar School became so impoverished, both by the competition from Tiffin Boys 'School and the plunder of its endowment funds that there was a move to close it altogether. It was only saved by the raising of a large public subscription.

It is tantalising that, because of the loss of the local Schoolwardens records and other documents, so little is known of Kingston schools in general until the eighteenth century. In 1528 Isabell Rothewood's will provided for the setting up of a "free schole . . . for the erudition and teaching of scholers there for ever" but stipulated that it must be established within three years of her death. We have no way of knowing if her wishes were carried out.

In 1557 Robert Hamonde left property "to sette upp a Free Grammar Schole in Kyngeston", possibly because of the dissolution of the Lovekyn Chantry Chapel and school. Presumably something was done for two years later, in 1559, Hamonde's widow left a legacy to "Edmund Greene, Scholemaster of the Free Grammar Schole of Kingston upon Temys".

There were charity schools in Kingston from a fairly early date. For example, Elizabeth Brown's will of 1648 provided for the Corporation to appoint a woman to teach poor children and put them out as apprentices. By 1852 this bequest was paying for the clothing and education of sixty boys and girls.

Edward Belitha left funds in 1717 to employ "some honest reputable woman . . . to teach twenty poor persons daughters to read and work plain work well". His legacy was so wisely invested that by the middle of the nineteenth century it was providing education for thirty children.

Thomas and John Tiffin, two wealthy Kingston brewers and brothers, instructed in their wills of 1638 and 1639 that the profits from certain investments should be used to educate "honest poore mens sonnes" at "some good schoole" and then bind them out as apprentices.

Corporation records between the seventeenth and nineteenth centuries show that many children benefited from these charities, and that as great a number as possible were given specialised trade training by being apprentices. The Chamberlains Accounts of 1603 mention: "Paid to Coxhale that taught the poore children of the towne to worke, for his wages 10s. 2d." In 1707 the *Bailiffs Minute Book* records that fifteen-year-old Elizabeth Mathews should be bound apprentice until the age of twenty-one and provided with "3 shiffts, 2 pairc of shooes and two pair of stockins. A pettecoate gowne, a pare of bodies, 3 caps and straw hatt, 3 aprons, 3 handkershiffs."

The *Court of Assembly Book* entries for 1722 include an order that the "6 boys of Mr. Tiffins Gift and the 6 girls on Mrs. Browns Gift, and the schoolmaster and schoolmistress belonging to them, be all summoned to appear before the Corporation to be examined about their Behaviour and the progress they have made in their learning".

All children in the Workhouse were taught reading, writing and arithmetic and went before the Trustees from time to time to demonstrate their progress "so that the Master and Scholars and others of the poor may have their due commendation" (*"Scheme for the Building of a Workhouse"*, Borough Archives *KG3/4/1*).

There were also some private schools in Kingston, including one opened by John Bauman, a Lutheran preacher, after he had fled from the religious persecution in Prague in 1626. This school was eventually taken over by the famous Presbyterian minister Daniel Mayo, who continued to run it until his death in 1733.

An important step forward for working children was made in 1798 when William Ranyard founded Kingston's first Sunday School in Brick Lane. The School, supported by voluntary donations, taught reading, writing and scripture to children who had to earn their living for the other six days of the week. Classes began at 9.30 each Sunday morning, and by 1817 seventy boys and sixty girls were attending.

During the nineteenth century Kingston's educational facilities were greatly increased. The first voluntary subscription school opened in Richmond Road in 1819, and was followed by the National School at Norbiton, the Bluecoat School in Wood Street and the Ragged School, held in a barn belonging to Kingston Bridge.

The *Surrey Comet*, reporting on a Christmas dinner given in the Ragged School in 1858, was impressed by the cleanliness of the 200 pupils—"even those without shoes had their feet clean".

In 1870 the Forster Act decreed that Board Schools should be set up by elected Local Boards in areas where there were insufficient voluntary schools. But Kingston's existing charity and church schools were judged to be adequate, and the town did not establish a Board. In 1876 the Sandon Act made school attendance compulsory for the first time, and also forbade the employment of children under ten. Kingston School Attendance Committee was formed in 1877 as a result of this Act. Ten years later, in addition to its Grammar and Tiffin Schools, the town could boast twelve elementary schools providing education for 4,873 children.

Some townspeople were angered by the cost of this subsidised education.

"As a general rule the best scholars make the best servants. We recommend this to the attention of those who object to educating the poor," declared the *Surrey Comet*.

Local Boards and School Attendance Committees were abolished by the Balfour Act of 1902 and their powers transferred to counties and county boroughs. Kingston, as a borough with more than

10,000 people, was classed as a Part III authority, which meant it could administer its own elementary schools and spend up to a penny rate on higher education.

Elementary schools remained until 1944. Then the three stages of Primary, Secondary and Further Education were established, and the term "elementary" was dropped. Part III Authorities also disappeared, and instead counties were divided into Divisional Executives—Kingston becoming part of the North Central Divisional Executive for Surrey.

However, Kingston became its own Educational Authority again in 1963 as a result of the London Government Act.

CHAPTER VIII

Church and Chapel

Kingston Church, and the green lawns which surround it, is a tranquil island amid the jostle and ceaseless traffic roar of modern Kingston.

On this spot Christians of every station, from powerful kings to the humblest serfs, have met together in worship for well over twelve centuries.

There has been a church here at least since 838. In that year the Saxon King Egbert held his great ecclesiastical council in Kingston, the results of which were so far-reaching that they survive today. Egbert's purpose was to strengthen his kingdom by forming an alliance with the Church. In return he could offer the protection of the most powerful king and kingdom in England, and the right of the bishops to rank as "spiritual lords" of the State—a right they still retain.

The first act of this important meeting was the presentation of land to the Archbishop. The gift was conveyed "before the altar" indicating that there was a church in Kingston at that time.

This is doubtless the church referred to in the Coronation Service of Ethelred II, crowned in Kingston in 978: "Two Bishops . . . shall lead the King to the church . . . when the King arrives at the church he shall prostrate himself before the altar . . ."

This church, known to have been dedicated to All Hallows, was almost certainly destroyed by the Danes who, in 1019, swept up the Thames as far as Staines, burning towns on both sides of the river as they went.

The only tantalising relic that remains is a fragment of a Saxon cross, thought to have formed part of a lofty churchyard cross, and whose marking indicates that it could date from as early as the seventh century. This fragment, now displayed in the church, was used as building material when the Norman church was constructed, but was excavated from the walls during nineteenth-century restoration work.

The Danes killed priests, robbed their churches, then set fire to them, leaving only the naked walls. So it is likely that when Gilbert the Norman built Kingston's cruciform Church of All Saints he followed the usual Norman practice of incorporating the old nave walls into the new building, and built the tower on arches on the site of the previous Saxon chancel. Thus the visitor who enters Kingston Church today, and stands under the central tower arches, may well be standing on the altar site of the Saxon Church of All Hallows, where kings were crowned and where the course of church history was changed in 838.

The Domesday Book of 1086 records that Kingston had a church. This doubtless refers to the ancient Chapel of St. Mary, which was built before Domesday and survived until the eighteenth century. It may have been built by the Danish King Canute, who became a Christian after winning the English throne, and built many churches as compensation for the destruction wrought earlier by the Danes. He is also known to have visited Kingston.

The Chapel adjoined the parish church on its south side, and was known locally as "the church of the coronations" because it contained paintings of Saxon kings being crowned in Kingston. Gilbert the Norman had presented the living of Kingston to Merton Priory, but after the dissolution of the Priory by Henry VIII in 1538 St. Mary's Chapel became the parish storehouse. Thus it remained until 1730 when the sexton, Abram Hammerton, carelessly undermined the foundations while gravedigging. Part of the building collapsed, killing him and another man. His daughter Hester was also trapped, but was rescued alive to succeed her father as sexton.

The remaining portion of the chapel was soon demolished by the parishioners, and the site left bare until 1825 when it was merged with the churchyard for burials and lost.

It was rediscovered in 1926 during excavations by Dr. Finny, who was Mayor of Kingston seven times, High Steward of the Borough, and a devoted local historian. Fragments from the ancient walls were rebuilt, and the site marked out with metal plaques.

The Chapel was sixty feet long and twenty-five feet wide, with walls two-and-a-half feet thick, and some of its floor tiles, discovered by Dr. Finny, are estimated to date from between 1030 and 1050. Historians have declared many times that Abram Hammerton deserved his fate for destroying what would have been one of the most interesting church buildings in England had it survived.

Meanwhile the rare old pictures, which were painted on wood and had hung in the chapel for centuries, were thought to have been lost for ever. However, Dr. Finny carried out an intensive search and eventually found pictures and fragments of paintings which had been used as wainscotting in the servants quarters of Baston Manor House in Kent. A Latin inscription on one of them showed that it came from Kingston. It now hangs in the home of the Society of Antiquaries in London, together with another picture and a fragment thought to come from the old chapel at Kingston.

Dishonesty and destruction has dogged the history of Kingston Church. Throughout the thirteenth and fourteenth centuries the greed of the Merton Priors milked most of its income, leaving only a pittance to maintain the building and pay the vicar. The Bishop of Winchester was forced to intervene several times, ordering the Priory to keep the church in proper repair and give the Vicar his rightful share of the income which, besides money from legacies, offerings and other sources, included tithes of grain, livestock, cheese, milk, honey and other produce from the parish.

The Priory evidently ignored these instructions, for in 1368 the Bishop issued a mandate stating that the chancel at Kingston was in a serious state of disrepair, though his predecessor had ordered the Priory to repair and re-roof it.

Perhaps it was due to this neglect that the original Norman nave was pulled down in the fourteenth century and entirely rebuilt on a wider plan.

The tower at this time was surmounted by a lofty wooden spire which was destroyed in 1445 when, says the seventeenth-century chronicler Stow: "On Candlemas eve in divers places of England was great weathering of wind, hayle, snow, rayne and thunders with lightening, whereby divers churches were sore shaken, and the steeple of Waltham in Essex and of Kingstone in Surrey was also fired by the same lightenings."

William of Worcester records the same event, adding that someone died in Kingston Church during the storm "through fear of a spirit which he saw there".

Robert Somerby, Vicar of Kingston from 1478 to 1501, bequeathed funds to rebuild the steeple, and a memorial inscription to him is still preserved on the tower: "Pray for the sole of Master Robert Somerby sometime Vicar of Kyngeston."

After the Reformation, and the dissolution of Merton Priory, the Kingston church fabric again began to deteriorate. To make matters worse Edward VI despatched commissioners to churches throughout the land to seize every item of value "to the King's use".

Kingston, a well-endowed church in a prosperous town, must have had much valuable plate, jewellery and robes. However, the plunder of the Royal commissioners was so thorough that when a second group of them was sent out their inventory—dated September 1552—stated that not a single article of plate was left in the church except two chalices and a crismatory, and all but a few of the oldest vestments had gone. Within a few months yet another set of commissioners visited the church. This time everything except the chalices had disappeared, but the commissioners noted that there remained "to the kinges use fyve great belles in the steple, a suns (sanctus) bell, and a chyme for the belles".

Worse indignities were to befall the church during the Civil Wars of the seventeenth century when Roundhead troops occupied Kingston. They used the church as a stable, smashed up the pews and destroyed many monuments and tablets.

It is hardly surprising that by 1699 the Church had deteriorated to such an extent that a vestry meeting reported that the building was almost ruinous. A rate of 6d. in the pound was levied on the parish to pay for repairs, but in 1703 a storm damaged the steeple so severely that in 1708 the Bishop authorised it to be taken down, together with the upper part of the tower. The steeple was never replaced, but the top portion of the tower was rebuilt in brick and decorated with a large stone pineapple.

Disaster threatened the tower again in 1971 when it was found to be in such a precarious condition that the Mayor launched a massive appeal for funds to save it.

The lower portion of the tower dates from the thirteenth century, and is the oldest part of the present church fabric. The rest of the building is described in the comprehensive little guide book on sale inside the church.

Mediaeval Kingston was such an active ecclesiastical centre that the Bishops of Winchester established their own residence near the church, on a site still known as Bishops Hall. But, as Leland relates in his *Itinerary*, they eventually abandoned it in favour of a new house at Esher, and the Kingston building was leased out as an ordinary dwelling.

Kingston has always been a centre for radical religious views and actions.

In 1331 the *Patent Rolls* of Edward III reveal that the Archdeacon of Surrey, William Inge, was attacked and imprisoned by forty-six Kingston men, including several fishermen.

In 1513 four Lollard reformers were tried at Kingston. Thomas Denys, who had a previous conviction for heresy, was burnt in the Market Place. Philip Braban, John Langborowe and Margery Japson, all described as Kingston artisans, escaped the flames by renouncing their dangerous beliefs.

During the Reformation one of the most enthusiastic Protestants was Richard Taverner, Henry VIII's Clerk of the Privy Seal. Both Cardinal Wolsey and Thomas Cromwell found him a useful ally in promoting the "new" English church, and he was granted a licence to preach. He also wrote religious works, including an English version of the Bible. He was duly rewarded in 1547 when Edward VI granted him much of the land and property that had belonged to the dissolved Lovekyn Chantry Chapel at Kingston.

Taverner managed to escape royal retribution by retiring to his Kingston estates when the Catholic Queen Mary Tudor came to the Throne, but he almost certainly used his influence and colourful personality to increase Protestant fervour in the town. He died in 1575, doubtless happy in the knowledge that a fanatical brand of Puritanism was being preached in Kingston Church by the Curate-in-Charge, John Udall. By 1588 Udall had been stripped of his preaching licence, and in 1591 he was sentenced to death for his revolutionary religious activities. He was reprieved, only to die in prison soon afterwards.

But Protestant fanaticism continued to smoulder in Kingston. In 1588 two Catholic priests, William Way and William Wigges, were hanged in the Market Place because of their religious opinions and in 1631 Dr. Edmund Staunton became Vicar of Kingston, a position he managed to retain for some twenty years—even though he was suspended from the ministry for a time in 1634 because of his Puritan views. These views led him to side with the Presbyterians during the Civil Wars, and he eventually became President of Corpus Christi College, Oxford. However, after the Restoration he was expelled from the church for his non-conformity.

Dr. Staunton left three lasting memorials in Kingston. One is the brass plaque in Kingston Church commemorating his ten children, all of whom died tragically in infancy. The others are the Congregational and Baptist churches in Kingston, both of which have their origins in the Presbyterian doctrines instilled by Dr. Staunton into Richard Mayo, his young clerical assistant.

In 1658 Mayo succeeded his master as Vicar of Kingston. He was happy and popular in his new position, though in the preface to his book on the life of Edmund Staunton he makes oblique reference to his quarrels with the more militant Quakers in the town:

> I have somewhat against some of you, but I won't reveal that upon the housetop.

In 1622, just before his annual income was due, Mayo was expelled from the Kingston living. He promptly began preaching to a little group of rebels from the parish church who held secret religious meetings in each other's houses. By 1669 the official Episcopal Returns noted that the group had grown to a hundred members.

In 1672 the Act of Indulgence meant that non-Conformists need no longer meet in secret. A house owned by John Pigot in Kingston was licensed as a Presbyterian meeting house with Mayo as its minister. He left in 1687 to work in London, but the Kingston group continued to flourish, and by about 1690 had its own meeting house in Brick Lane (later re-named Union Street after a Baptist Union Church had been established there). The religious ideals laid down by Staunton and Mayo received fresh impetus in 1698 when Richard Mayo's famous son, Daniel Mayo, took over the Kingston Presbyterian ministry. He served there until his death in 1733. However, the congregation dwindled under his successor. George Whightwick. There were disagreements, and in 1775 the members split, one group eventually founding a Baptist Church in Brick Lane and the other a Congregational Church in Eden Street.

But the oldest non-conformist group in Kingston were the Quakers. George Fox, founder of the movement, came here many times and by the 1650s members were holding well-attended meetings at the home of a Kingston meal merchant, John Fielder, who occupied part of the building known as King John's Dairy.

Kingston Quakers were heavily fined, and sometimes beaten for their beliefs. Nevertheless, they gained strong support from local businessmen and in 1663 were able to buy land in London Road for a burial ground. Ten years later their present Meeting House in Eden Street was built.

Methodist preachers were also struggling to win converts in Kingston by the middle of the eighteenth century. They found the task difficult and dangerous. Years of religious tolerance had made the church members slack and complacent while the majority of people in Kingston had become indifferent, even hostile, to religion.

In 1760, for instance, a Methodist preacher had gathered a large crowd around him in Kingston when he was set upon by a mob and there was a riot which had to be quelled by Dragoons quartered in the town.

The Reformation, and the steady increase in Puritan influence did much to subdue the festive vitality which for centuries had made Kingston Parish Church the very centre of the people's lives—not only for worship, but for the relaxation and jollity which were considered to be an equally important part of Christian life. Parish records up to the seventeenth century are full of references to games, dances, plays and other merriment with refreshments always on hand.

For example, in the Churchwardens' Accounts:

1538: A killderkyn of bere dronken in the m'kett place, 1s.
1570: Item payd for drynke for the quyer on festevall days, 16d.

Kingston Corporation retained a strongly Puritan outlook until comparatively recent times. A *Court of Assembly Book* entry for 20 November 1850 records the unanimous decision of the members to send an Address to the Queen, and to insert statements in The Times and the Morning Herald, "viewing with indignation the late insidious attempts of the Papal See to establish its spiritual dominion in this country" and condemning the "aggression and encroaching Policy of the Bishop of Rome".

Four years earlier Alexander Raphael, a former MP and owner of the Surbiton Park Estate, had shown what he thought of such attitudes by building his own Roman Catholic chapel overlooking the river on the Portsmouth Road. He chose an ornate Italian style, and in what disapproving locals considered to be a tasteless lauding of his own surname, dedicated the building to St.

Raphael. Until then the nearest Roman Catholic church had been at Brentford.

St. Raphael's still stands today, and is one of the Borough's Listed Buildings. Meanwhile Kingston Parish Church is endeavouring to revive its ancient role as the pivot of people's everyday living. The building is no longer reserved exclusively for prayers and formal worship, but is also used for fairs, suppers and other social gatherings.

Until 1842, when St. Peter's Church was built at Norbiton, All Saints was the only Anglican Church serving the huge parish of Kingston, so farmers from the surrounding countryside had a long walk to Divine Service. The nineteenth-century local historian F. S. Merryweather recalled that the men wore Sunday smocks, carefully pleated and embroidered by their wives, while their womenfolk wore red cloaks and straw hats, and clattered up the aisle on wooden pattens. In earlier centuries so many worshippers brought their sheepdogs and turnspit dogs with them that there was a church officer known as the Dog-Whipper. His task was to eject troublesome animals from the church, and he was armed with a whip and large wooden tongs for the purpose. Kingston's dog-whipper is frequently referred to in the Churchwardens' Accounts up to the seventeenth century. For example:

1567: Paid the whypper of the dogges howll yer. 17d.
1578: To wright for beating the dogges out of the churche, for halfe a yeare 6d.

Meanwhile the aristocracy of the town, having driven to church in their carriages, sat aloof with the doors of their high-backed pews firmly shut. Until late in the sixteenth century all worshippers sat on forms, regardless of their rank. But in 1585 the Bailiffs and other town dignitaries met in the church and decided "that ye seats in ye church shall be altred and the psshioners to be placed in order in their degrees and callinges".

Members of the Corporation had their own seats in front of the congregation. In 1629, for instance, the Churchwardens paid 11s. "for mending the doore and desks before the XV head boroughs".

The floor of the church was covered in straw. In fact, when Queen Elizabeth's High Admiral, Edward Fynes, took a lease on the Rectory of Kingston in 1567 the *Calendar of Patent Rolls* show that one of the terms of the agreement was that he must "provide straw yearly for the Church and Chapel of Kingeston . . . with carriage thereof, as accustomed".

In 1635 the Churchwardens paid 3s. for a pewter chamber pot for use in church, while over the years many "hower glasses" and "½ hower glasses" were purchased as reminders to over-zealous preachers.

For centuries the town's fire engines occupied a prominent place in the south chancel, and the Vestry Minutes of 1695 direct that "the engines belonging to this town be constantly set there" as usual.

However, by 1836 the appliance was in such disrepair that the Churchwardens agreed to let the Corporation take custody of it—provided they paid a shilling a year in rent. But fire-fighting methods remained primitive, and it was not until 1910 that Kingston Corporation, after much hesitation, decided to replace its antiquated, horse-drawn fire engine with one powered by internal combustion.

Until the middle of the nineteenth-century Church Rates were levied throughout the parish. The result was an annual "civil war" between the Non-Conformists and Anglicans, and feelings eventually ran so high that Ald Frederick Gould, who was a churchwarden, introduced a system of pew rents. This raised enough money to abolish church rates for good.

The importance of Kingston Church, and the value of its living, is illustrated by the fact that until 1769 the churches at Richmond, Petersham, East Molesey and Thames Ditton were, to the intense irritation of their congregations, merely dependent chapelries belonging to Kingston Church. From its earliest years Kingston had formed part of the Diocese of Winchester, but in 1877, as a result of the Bishopric of St. Albans Act, the parish was transferred to the Rochester Diocese. In 1905 it was moved again to form part of the newly-created Diocese of Southwark, and a Suffragan Bishop of Kingston was appointed.

9. London Road, Kingston, showing one of the sensational new covered-top trams introduced to the town in 1906. After only a year they were replaced by cheaper, roofless models. The furniture shop on the left, replaced by the Elite Picture Theatre in 1902, is now the site of the C & A store.

Clarence Street,   Kingston-on-Thames.

10. Clarence Street, photographed from its junction with Eden Street, in 1900. On the right is the Kings Arms, a busy staging house for the Windsor, Guildford and Box Hill coaches.

CHAPTER IX

Bricks and Mortar

For centuries Kingston has been too energetically living the present and planning the future to put much value on the past. Yet at least 5,000 years of history lies behind this hard-headed town, much of it now lost for ever. With such a story to tell, but so little left with which to illustrate it, Kingston is at once a source of fascination and frustration to the historian.

It is a depressing fact that in the whole Royal Borough of Kingston upon Thames there are only twenty-eight listed buildings, five of which are churches, four conduit houses, two bridges and two pieces of stone. Yet planners are eager to make still further inroads into this meagre legacy.

These and other truths were presented to a Department of the Environment Inspector in 1971 during successful opposition to Corporation proposals to demolish Picton House, an eighteenth-century house on the river bank in High Street. Many people were shocked to learn that Kingston has fewer historic buildings than any other borough south of the Thames, and that in the whole of the Greater London area there are only three Boroughs with fewer—Barking, Brent and Newham.

In a town so stripped of what was once a wealth of historic architecture, archaeological discoveries are of particular value.

In recent years archaeologists have found evidence of a riverside tribe living in Kingston in about 3500 B.C. The clues were unearthed in 1965 during site preparations for the building of the multi-storey car park in Eden Street, and included pottery, bison horns and deer antlers, thought to be Neolithic, and approximately 5,500 years old. The discoveries were made in what was probably the old bed of the Hogsmill River, indicating a riverside settlement of people who threw their refuse into the water. A bank of the old river course was also unearthed, together with a number of "pot-boilers"—stones which were heated, then dropped into the contents of pots to heat them.

Bronze Age implements dating from about 2000 B.C. and Iron

99

Age pottery of around 650 B.C. have been found on Kingston Hill and the bed of the Thames, and can be seen in Kingston Museum.

There is an interesting theory, accepted for centuries, but questioned by modern archaeologists, that the Romans built the fortress town of Thamesa on Kingston Hill to guard the vital river crossing. The local historian Biden quotes Gale's *Itinerary* in support of this idea, while Leland's *Itinerary*, compiled in the first half of the sixteenth century, declares that Roman foundations and coins were frequently unearthed on the hill by ploughmen in Tudor times, while only a few years earlier remains of a Roman mint had been found with "much Romayne money of sylver, and plates of silver to coyne, and brasses to bete into plates to coyne, and chaynes of sylver".

If Thamesa did exist here it presumably fell into decay after the Romans left Britain, for Leland states that the Saxons built a new town and a bridge and "toke from the very clive of Combe parke side to build on the Tamise side". This town was known as Moreford, and Biden asserts that it was the first town to be built in Britain after the Saxon invasion. He also supports the tradition that Moreford was destroyed during a savage invasion by the Danes, and that the town was rebuilt further up the river on its present site.

Kingston's most famous monument is the slab of grey sandstone which stands outside the Guildhall. This is reputed to be the Coronation Stone on which at least seven Saxon kings were crowned, but its origins are a mystery which has fascinated archaeologists for years. It is generally believed to have formed part of an ancient Druids circle, similar to that of Stonehenge, and there is a theory that pre-historic Kingston was such a sacred spot that, centuries later, the Saxon kings chose to be crowned here rather than in their capital town of Winchester.

The stone, now one of Kingston's proudest possessions, seems to have been regarded as an awkward encumbrance in previous centuries. The *Court of Assembly Book* contains an entry for 22 April 1703 that "the Square smooth stone in Court Hall be delivered to Mr. Bayliffe Reeves to make an Inscription there on for ye Free Gramer School". However, by 1724 the Court of Assembly is directing the Chamberlain to "forthwith remove the Pebble Stone that now lyes near Doctor Cranmer's doores" and put it under the Court Hall "there to remayne till further orders".

The stone was later relegated to the Saxon Chapel of St. Mary, which was then used as the parish storehouse, and was known to have been in the building when part of it collapsed. In 1825, after years spent lying somewhere near the church, it was placed beside the old Elizabethan Guildhall and used as a public mounting block. When the Guildhall was rebuilt in 1838–40 the stone was moved to the Assize Courts yard, and used as a mounting block by the County Magistrates.

It was saved by Ald. F. Gould who, shocked by the town's indifference towards one of its most interesting relics, raised £450 to have it mounted on a plinth, enclosed by Saxon style railings and put in a prominent place in the road near the Market in September 1850. A medal was struck to mark the occasion, a public holiday was granted, and thousands gathered to watch the Mayor, Mr. William Pamphilon, unveil the stone.

Then there was a Masonic ceremony during which the Provincial Grand Master of the Freemasons of Surrey anointed the slab with corn oil and wine. The British Museum showed its approval by giving a coin from the reign of each of the seven Kings known to have been crowned in Kingston, and these were set into the plinth.

The stone, which now stands near the Guildhall, was put under police guard in 1950 when the Stone of Scone was stolen from Westminster Abbey and there were warnings that the Kingston stone would be seized as well. There were similar threats in 1953 and, again, a police guard was mounted.

Heedlessness and neglect almost robbed Kingston of another of its most famous treasures. The fourteenth-century Lovekyn Chapel in London Road, unique as the only separate chantry chapel in England to survive the religious policies of Henry VIII and Edward VI, suffered such gross neglect that by 1878, when it no longer housed the ancient Kingston Grammar School, massive baulks of timber had to be placed against its walls to prevent their collapse. Most townspeople regarded it as a tiresome anachronism, and attempts to set up a restoration fund failed miserably. The building was about to be demolished when the Surrey Archaeological Society and the Society for the Preservation of Ancient Monuments intervened. They backed a vigorous campaign which eventually raised sufficient money for the restoration and re-opening of the chapel in 1886. It is now used as a junior library for Kingston Grammar School.

The Chapel is dedicated to St. Mary Magdalene, and was

founded in 1309 by Edward Lovekyn, member of an old Kingston family. No one could endow a chantry at that time without the express permission of the King, and it is thought that Lovekyn was so favoured because in 1299—when he was Bailiff of Kingston, and Edward I had visited the town at least twice (*Calendar of Letters Patent*, 23 February and 8 March)—he had provided the feast at the betrothal of the King to Margaret of France. This left him £500 out of pocket, but it was agreed that he should receive the fee farm rent from Kingston in payment (*Calendar of Patent Rolls*, 15 April 1300). However, Kingston had been assigned to the Queen as part of her dower seven months previously (*Calendar of Patent Rolls*, 10 Sept 1299) and ten years later Lovekyn was still waiting for his money.

The matter was finally settled by Edward II in 1309, and the licence for the chapel was granted the same year.

Chantry chapels were not intended for public worship. They were private buildings in which resident chaplains were paid to pray and say Mass daily for the souls of the founder and his family. Thus the Lovekyn chapel, though small by modern standards, was quite large enough for its original purpose.

Edward Lovekyn died soon after the consecration of his chapel in 1310, leaving land and money for its maintenance. But his son Robert apparently misappropriated this endowment and neglected the chapel to such an extent that he was excommunicated. By 1352 the chapel was in ruins, and only another endowment could save it from extinction. Fortunately John Lovekyn, Edward's son by a second marriage, determined that his father's religious intentions should be fulfilled. He was a wealthy man, who served four times as Lord Mayor of London, and in 1352 he rebuilt the Chapel and gave it a generous endowment.

John Lovekyn directed that Edward III and his Queen Philippa should be included in the prayers offered at his Chapel, and head carvings of the King and Queen survive on two brackets set in the East window. Two subsidiary chapels dedicated to St. Anne and St. Loye originally adjoined the building (see *Calendar of Patent Rolls*, 1 March 1561) but no trace of these remains.

John Lovekyn died in 1368 and his widow married Sir William Walworth, who had been one of her husband's apprentices. Sir William, who became famous as the man who slew Wat Tyler, leader of the Peasants' Revolt of 1381, increased the endowments of the Chapel in 1371 and added a second Chaplain. No other endowments are recorded before the Chantries Act of 1547 abolished the foundation completely. All the Chapel's wealth was seized by the Crown, but restored by Queen Elizabeth in 1561 when she decreed that the Chapel and its endowments should be used for the founding and maintenance of "the free grammar school of Queen Elizabeth" (*Calendar of Patent Rolls*, 1 March 1561).

However, the profit-seeking motives of Kingston's nineteenth-century tradesmen resulted in the destruction of a fine old building whose origins were even older than those of the Lovekyn Chapel. This was King John's Dairy, which stood in the High Street, but was demolished amid protests in 1885 to make way for some minor shops. It was reputed to be part of farm buildings belonging to a palace built in Kingston by King John at the end of the twelfth century, and Biden relates that during the mid-nineteenth century a beam of solid Spanish chestnut was discovered in the building with the date 1201 carved into it.

The "Dairy" became famous in later years as the place where George Fox, founder of the Quaker movement, preached many of his early sermons in 1650.

The only remains of the palace itself is a piece of early thirteenth-century carved pillaring which stands on a plinth outside Kingston Library. There is no trace at all of the royal residence used by the Saxon kings, and thought to have stood near The Bittoms.

Another nineteenth-century casualty was the mediaeval tithe barn at Canbury, used for threshing and storing the Vicar's share of all the grain grown in the parish. It was one of the largest barns in Britain, with enough room for twenty wagons to be unloaded under its roof simultaneously, and its red, high-pitched roof was a familiar landmark above the hedgerows. In 1843 it was sold by public auction for £160 and immediately pulled down. Its site is now covered by Kingston Railway Station.

In 1838 the old Town Hall, which had stood in the Market Place since the early sixteenth century, was pulled down and replaced by the present structure. The old Hall, thought to have been an Elizabethan restoration of a far older building, was quaintly gabled, and mounted on timber pillars to provide an open market space beneath. It was enlarged during the reign of Queen Anne to provide extra accommodation for the Assizes, and sculptor Francis

Bird was paid £47 10s. to carve the gilded statue of Queen Anne which still looks out over the Market Place today.

Still the old building was hopelessly inadequate for court sittings, and the judges complained so bitterly that in 1808 the Corporation obtained an Act of Parliament authorising them to enclose and sell their common lands to pay for a new Town Hall. The Kingston Enclosure Act wrought great changes in Kingston by transforming tracts of open countryside, such as Norbiton and Surbiton Commons, into building sites. But it took thirty years to negotiate all the enclosures, and in the meantime the judges were becoming so angry that in 1811 the Corporation built new Assize Courts at the South end of the Market Place. These were demolished to make way for the present Guildhall, opened in 1935 by Princess Alice, Countess of Athlone.

By 1838 the Corporation was ready to pull down the sixteenth-century Town Hall and replace it with a new building designed by Charles Henman. It was completed in 1840, and remained the town's civic centre until the opening of the new Guildhall. Today, stripped of its former panelling, stained glass and handsome fireplaces, it is used as the Market House.

One of Kingston's most tantalising archaeological secrets is the whereabouts of the castle that the mighty Earl of Warwick is reputed to have held in the town.

Local tradition asserts that it stood at what is now the junction of Eden Street with Clarence Street, and modern offices nearby have been named Warwick House and Neville House to commemorate the earl. But it had vanished by the seventeenth century when the historian John Aubrey visited the town, and the question remains: was it a true castle, or just a stronghold to guard the bridge and the approach from London? Biden records that a few years before he wrote his history of Kingston in 1852 building work on the traditional castle site revealed massive underground vaults, but they were converted into sewers before archaeologists could examine them.

Until quite recent times Kingston had such a wealth of ancient buildings that it could afford to take them for granted. Within a half-mile radius of the church was a mass of alleys, lanes and courtyards, their heavily-timbered houses dating back to Tudor and Stuart times. North of the church, between Wood Street and the river, almost all the houses were original Tudor structures. They were occupied by fishermen and bargees, and here and there were ancient alehouses occupied by both Royalist and Roundhead troops during the Civil Wars.

This area, known as the Back Lanes and The Horsefair, was well preserved until Victorian times. But Ayliffe recalled in his *Recollections*, compiled in 1914, that the buildings began to degenerate, and the authorities became so lax that they would grant liquor licences to anyone able to produce three guineas. Drinking houses sprang up in such profusion that the once delightfully picturesque streets became a hotbed of vice, full of squalid lodging houses and a colony of Italian organ grinders. The whole area was cleared in 1905.

The life of the Back Lanes, and the general topography of the town, was considerably altered when Kingston Bridge was moved some fifty yards upstream in 1825. Until then the coach road from London to the West Country ran from London Road, down Wood Street into the Horsefair, then west down what is now Old Bridge Street and over the flimsy wooden structure that for centuries—until the opening of Putney Bridge in 1729—was the first Thames bridge above London.

The first documentary reference to Kingston Bridge is dated 1219, though it obviously existed well before then, and down the centuries it was in a constant state of disrepair, the Corporation frequently having to provide a ferry when the bridge was impassable. In 1812 the bridge was beyond repair, and its endowments were unable to meet rebuilding costs. The Corporation's claim that the counties of Surrey and Middlesex should bear the burden was legally rejected. The Corporation was therefore forced to raise money by selling land, and in 1825 the Prime Minister, Lord Liverpool, laid the first stone of a new bridge a little further upstream from the old one. It was completed in 1828 and opened by the Duchess of Clarence, afterwards Queen Adelaide. The new approach road to the bridge was named Clarence Street in her honour.

Tolls were charged on every person or vehicle crossing the new bridge, and caused considerable financial hardship to many of the townspeople. These tolls were farmed out to the highest bidder at regular public lettings, business being conducted with the aid of a sandglass. As soon as bidding slackened the sandglass was turned, and if no higher bid had been made by the time the sand ran out, the last bidder became owner of the tolls.

Alderman Gould determined to abolish this system, and it was mainly through his efforts that the Government eventually gave a grant for freeing the bridge. The freeing ceremony was performed by the Lord Mayor of London on 12 March 1850. The old toll gate was lifted from its hinges, placed on a trolley and drawn across the bridge to Hampton Wick before being publicly burnt.

In 1914 the bridge was widened on the upstream side. This time the County Councils of Middlesex and Surrey paid the bill, but there was no opening ceremony because of the outbreak of World War I.

An interesting précis history of Kingston Bridge is set out on a plaque on one of the parapets.

Kingston, because of its close connections with malting and brewing, has always been eager to enjoy good ale. The *Bailiffs Minute Book* and other contemporary records indicate that by the eighteenth century there was approximately one alehouse to every fifty inhabitants. These, together with most of Kingston's fine old inns, have either been demolished or rebuilt since Victorian times.

The Fighting Cocks in London Road had stables used by the Southampton and Portsmouth coaches, and when it was rebuilt the remains of two circular cock-fighting pits were found in the yard. Nearby, on the other side of the road, was the Jolly Sailors, whose extensive stabling was used by many trade vans and coaches.

However, the biggest range of stabling in the town was at the Druids Head, which still stands in the Market Place.

In Clarence Street was the Kings Arms, where the Box Hill, Windsor and Guildford coaches changed horses. A magnificent old inn was The Castle, now occupied by Hide's store in the Market Place. However, the inn's fine early seventeenth-century staircase has been retained in the store, while its eighteenth-century outside gallery survived until the main part of the present building was constructed in 1912. The Sun, noted for its ballroom and fine riverside gardens, was pulled down in 1931 to make way for Woolworth's.

The Griffin, built in the reign of Edward VI, was the business and political hub of Kingston throughout the nineteenth century. It still occupies its prominent site near the Market Place, though its once famous gilded front has been replaced by a Victorian facade.

Between the Griffin and Clattern Bridge stood The Crane, reputed to have been built in the reign of Edward II, and Kingston's most important inn during the sixteenth and seventeenth centuries. The *Calendars of State Papers* reveal that important ambassadors and members of the Royal Court lodged there, while the Parliamentarians chose it as their county Military HQ during the Civil Wars of the seventeenth century. By the nineteenth century the inn had been re-named the Jolly Butchers, and had taken on a more commonplace character. Ayliffe recalls that four sets of post horses waited outside the inn in the 1830s, often accompanied by a fish van laden with Worthing mackerel. When the van arrived the town crier would go round the streets announcing that new mackerel was now available at three or four for a shilling.

In later years this historic inn became a restaurant, known as Ye Olde Post House. An old window where the mailbags were handed in survived to the end, together with the "wig room" where eighteenth century gentlemen retired to powder their hair. This marvellous old building was demolished in 1954 on the grounds that its beams were unsafe.

An even greater loss was the Old Malt House, which stood on the left side of the High Street going towards Portsmouth. This sixteenth-century building, Kingston's last remaining malthouse, received a Building Preservation Order in 1965. One Sunday morning, only six weeks later, it was illegally demolished.

One of the oldest buildings in the Market Place is a modest little fifteenth-century timber framed house that now forms part of Boots. Ironically, this genuine fragment of history is eclipsed by the mock antiquity of the rest of Boots' facade. Visitors gaze at its attractively old-world timbers, gables, inscriptions and statues—usually unaware that it is a twentieth-century creation.

In the High Street, just beyond the Market Place, is Clattern Bridge, the oldest bridge in Surrey and one of the oldest in Britain.

A bridge was built on the site by the Saxons more than 1,000 years ago. However, in about 1180 this bridge was replaced by a stone structure of three arches, each with a span of twelve feet. These arches can still be seen beneath the parapet, and are a fine example of twelfth-century craftsmanship. The bridge, once only eight feet in width, has been considerably widened. But the original arches still carry a quarter of the width of the present roadway. The bridge was originally known as Clatrung Bridge, Clatrung being a Saxon word for clattering. It was subsequently known as Clattering Bridge, the name being corrupted to Clattern during the last century.

Cardinal Wolsey believed that the pure springs which rose on Coombe and Kingston Hills could alleviate kidney stones, and in 1516 he had the water brought to his new palace at Hampton Court through lead conduit pipes, which stretched three and a half miles across country, and passed under Kingston and the Thames. The three Tudor brick conduit houses still survive though Ivy Conduit, which stands in the garden of a Convent in George Road, was severely damaged in the last war. Gallows Conduit stands in an adjoining garden while Coombe Conduit is on the edge of Coombe Wood Golf Course, near Coombe Lane West. Two of these conduit houses have been given free to Kingston Corporation, who plan to keep them permanently preserved.

There were also a number of intermediate inspection points on Wolsey's water course, known as tamkins. All have vanished save one which stands on Coombe Wood Golf Course.

The twentieth century has done little to beautify the town of Kingston. However, two projects should be mentioned. One was the Market Place Improvement Scheme, which so enlivened the look of the Market that it won a commendation in the Civic Trust Competition of 1963. The other is the massive re-development that is planned during the next few years. It is hoped to open up the waterfront, provide more pedestrian precincts and restore some of the beauty which, considering its superb natural setting, is the true birthright of the town.

CHAPTER X

Modern Times

The bells that pealed out in Kingston in 1837 to welcome Victoria to the English throne were ringing in an era that was to annihilate the life the town had always known. Not that the townspeople had any inkling of it then. For on the day that Queen Victoria was proclaimed from the Market Place Kingston was much as it had been for centuries: a picturesque rural town surrounded by farmland, and with comfortable profits from malting, coaching and the wharving industry.

Coaching was at its peak, with more than twenty coaches using Kingston as the first stage post in the journey from London to the south and west. They included the *Rocket*, which changed at the Robin Hood in Kingston Vale and in 1821 achieved the journey to Portsmouth in nine hours. The *Royal Blue* went to Portsmouth too, while the *Red Rover*, *Royal William* and *The Times* jolted over Kingston's appalling roads on their way to Southampton. *The Diligent*, bound for Mouschill, and *The Sussex*, en route to Littlehampton, also rumbled through Kingston and helped to bring prosperity to its coaching inns.

There were local stage coaches, which made return trips from London every day, and six Royal Mail coaches going to and from Kingston and London daily. Their horses and coachmen were supplied by a contractor, and the coaches and guards by the Postmaster-General. Time was of vital importance to the mails, and the red-coated guards were issued with pistols, cutlasses, blunderbusses and a specially sealed chronometer.

Kingston's first Post Office had been established in the Market Place in 1716 when the *Bailiffs Minute Book* records that "Mr. William Patterson tooke the oath for the faithful discharge of his office of imployment as Postmaster within the towne of Kingston-on-Thames according to the Statute made in ye 9th yeare of her late Majestie's reign". But the initial nature of the enterprise is indicated by the fact that the Deputy Postmaster of the town, Joseph Johnson, was totally illiterate, unable even to sign his name.

Until 1837, and for some years afterwards, there was only one letter carrier to serve the whole town. In 1837 the job was held by William Rich, but when he became too feeble his wife Elizabeth took over, and was so conscientious that even when the town was flooded she found a boat and delivered her letters through house windows, refusing to leave until the correct fee had been paid. For stamps were not introduced until 1840, and letters had to be paid for on delivery. Some came by Twopenny Post from London, but others from further afield could cost the recipient 6d. or 8d. Postcards were introduced in 1871, though many Kingston people were outraged by their vulgar lack of privacy.

By 1875 the introduction of a cheap postal system, and the increase in local population caused largely by the railways, brought such a vast growth in business that Kingston Post Office was transferred to its present site in Brook Street. By then forty-seven active postmen had replaced the efforts of one old lady, and there were five deliveries a day instead of only one.

Kingston in the early Victorian age was vividly described by Ald. Frederick Gould in a series of interviews which later appeared in the *Surrey Comet* of 28 July 1900 as part of his obituary.

Gould, who served two terms as Mayor of Kingston and was one of the most forcefully efficient officers the Corporation had ever known, came to Kingston in 1839 and found it

a delightfully situated, quaint old town. Many of the houses were then ancient, half-timbered Elizabethan dwellings with overhanging bedrooms. Malthouses were visible in all directions, and everywhere one turned there were inland revenue officers. Many of the maltsmen at that time were credited with having made large fortunes by evading the revenue officers.

Some of the principal malthouses were in Back Lanes, High Street, The Bittoms and Surbiton Road. The old maltsmen were to be seen about the streets in their skull caps, knee breeches and worsted stockings, and every day they did their full share of hard work by the side of their men.

Surbiton was merely a far-flung portion of the ancient parish of Kingston, known for centuries as Towns End.

The introduction of railways completely changed this picture. In 1837 Kingston had thirty-eight flourishing malthouses and some of the best coaching inns in the country. By early 1840 no fewer than seventeen malthouses had closed while the remainder, together with many of the inns, had begun their long, and ultimately hopeless struggle to survive. Meanwhile the formerly ignored Towns End was emerging from its pretty country anonymity with a building and development programme which was to give it independent status and lead to the virtual eclipse of Kingston for several years.

This catastrophic blow to Kingston's trade was due not only to the development of the railways themselves, but also to Kingston's blind refusal to recognise that trains must inevitably supersede coaches and barges. The Corporation, largely influenced by coaching interests, roundly repudiated plans put forward by the London and Southampton Railway Company to run its new line through the town. Instead the Company was forced to by-pass Kingston by making an expensive cutting through Surbiton Hill and placing their so-called Kingston Station there. The original station was a small structure in the cutting near Ewell Road Bridge, and it was moved to its present site in 1840.

The trial trip on the new line was made from Vauxhall on 12 May 1838. Crowds thronged Kingston Station to see the steam coaches go by, the more adventurous passengers perching on the roof and holding their hats as the train sped along at the unprecedented rate of twenty m.p.h. Afterwards there was a grand banquet at which the Mayor of Kingston was conspicuously absent, and the station opened for normal service a few days later.

The trains were very different from those of today. First-class coaches were so long and narrow inside that luggage had to be strapped to the roof. Second-class coaches had bare seats and open, unsashed windows that made umbrellas necessary in wet weather. Third-class coaches were simply open trucks fitted with crude benches. The guard sat on the roof working a primitive brake, and was often so numb with exposure by the end of a journey that he had to be helped from his seat.

But the railway was an immediate success. Surbiton, when the station opened, consisted almost entirely of fields and parkland with only four houses and a windmill on Surbiton Hill. By 1852 there were 2,800 people living in 300 houses, and by 1887 there were 2,000 houses and a population of 10,500.

Meanwhile Kingston—which in 1841 could boast of being the second largest town in Surrey with 8,147 inhabitants—suffered serious economic deterioration. Stage coaching was dead, the last mail coach had left London in 1846 and many fine inns were ruined as a result. Retail trade was in decline, and the once-rich maltings were dying because grain was now being railed direct to London instead of first coming to Kingston by river.

By 1852 the historian W. D. Biden was writing that "Kingston is altogether more distinguished for what it has not than for what it has". It was a bitter experience for the Corporation to see the railway they had repudiated bring such prosperity to Surbiton. Their chagrin was increased at hearing this formerly insignificant part of the parish referred to as "New Kingston" or "Kingston-on-Railway", and by seeing a similar rise in the fortunes of nearby Richmond, whose Windsor Line station had opened in 1846.

The Corporation fought hard to have Surbiton brought within its Borough boundaries, but the new town successfully resisted. Its history of self-government began with the Surbiton Improvement Act of 1855 which set up an Improvement Commission. In 1894 this became the Urban District Council, which in turn became the Borough of Surbiton in 1936. There is a touch of historic irony in the fact that in 1965, as a result of the London Government Act passed two years earlier, Surbiton and Kingston were merged administratively with Malden and Coombe to become the London Borough of Kingston upon Thames.

Kingston Corporation, its lesson learned, worked feverishly throughout the 1850s to get the town a central station. Finally, in 1859, a branch from Twickenham on the Windsor Line was proposed. The South West Railway Kingston Extension Bill passed the House of Lords in 1860 and Kingston New Town Station, as it was called initially, opened on 1 January 1863 to great rejoicing and a celebration dinner at the Griffin. But the route to London was devious and slow, and in 1865 permission was granted for an extension to Wimbledon via Malden, opened in 1869. The line from Twickenham to Malden has been known ever since as the Kingston Loop. A new, high-level station had to be built to accommodate the new route, but this was subsequently re-designed in 1931–5 to provide the Kingston Station that stands today.

The Corporation then turned its attention to "Street Railways", already introduced in America, and beginning to fire British enthusiasm during the 1860s. In 1871 the first Bill to allow trams in Kingston was laid before Parliament. The proposed line was to be called Kew, Richmond and Kingston-on-Thames Tramways, and was to run from Richmond to Kingston Market Place. But

Parliament rejected the idea, and the town had to be temporarily content with horse-drawn buses. The first of these was introduced to Kingston in 1875 by a Mr. Stickland, who ran a small, one-horse bus from the Market Place to Surbiton. The fare was threepence, and the service operated twice an hour. It proved so popular that Mr. Stickland organised another service to Long Ditton, and other routes were opened up elsewhere in the town.

Horse-drawn cabs had already been popular for years. In fact, Kingston's last horse cab remained in service until 1932 when Mr. George Sketes retired after thirty-six years on the cab rank at Norbiton Station, while the old cabbies' shelter on Clattern Bridge was not removed until 1938.

Roads in Victorian Kingston were in such a state that passengers had to endure intense discomfort. Kingston's streets were not asphalted until 1880. Some were cobbled, with refuse and pools of fetid water stagnating between the stones. Others were dirt tracks, presenting quagmires in winter and deep, hard-baked ruts in summer. The road past Norbiton Church was particularly bad, and laden vehicles were often trapped in the mud for hours at a time.

Oil Mill Lane, now Villiers Road, was a narrow lane with hedges and ditches leading through "The Marsh" to Surbiton. The whole route was so thick with mud that it became impassable in wet weather. Hawks Road was just a country track—named after Hawks Farm—with its south side covered with fields of wheat, barley and wurzels. London Road was so narrow that two coaches could barely pass. Coombe Lane was a lonely, unlit lane, overhung with trees, where only the bravest ventured after dark and, once past Acre Road, Richmond Road passed between uninterrupted hedges and corn fields all the way to Ham.

A soaring population and the desire for modern transport caused Kingston Corporation to review its roads, and many new thoroughfares were made. The first and most significant of these was St. James's Road, built early in the 1850s to give easy access to Surbiton Station. Gordon Road and Canbury Park Road were laid across an extensive stretch of pasture known as Bull Fields; Birkenhead Avenue was driven through the stately grounds of Norbiton Hall; Queen Elizabeth Road opened in 1879; Kingston Hall Road was cut through nursery gardens, and opened in 1883 with a fanfare of trumpets and a civic procession. Fife Road curved across Jacksons Nurseries to provide a direct route from Clarence Street to the railway station.

It was the start of a building and redevelopment programme that has continued in varying degrees right up to the present. For by 1887 Kingston's population had swelled to 37,000—an increase of nearly 30,000 in fifty years—and new estates of terraced houses girdled the town and clustered round the railway station.

The Kingston Improvement Act of 1888 empowered the Corporation to levy £67,000 for further street improvements, including the building of a new bridge—the Springfield Road Bridge—over the Hogsmill River. The Act also authorised the Corporation to make compulsory purchase orders on various lands so the sites could be cleared for street alterations. This included all the land lying between Wood Street, Water Lane, Old Bridge Street, Thames Street and The Horsefair, much of which was occupied by the most squalid slums in the town.

During the first quarter of the twentieth century the heavy increase in motor traffic became a serious problem in Kingston. In 1913 a count was made of all the vehicles passing a selected point on the Portsmouth Road. A similar count was taken in 1925, and showed an increase of 125 per cent in the traffic passing through the town. Urgent action was essential, and early in 1924 Surrey County Council began building the Kingston Bypass. It was opened by the Prime Minister, Mr. Stanley Baldwin, on 28 October 1927, and made history as the first bypass road in Britain.

In 1883 the Corporation made another effort to secure a tramways system. This time the proposal was for a comprehensive service to be run jointly by the Corporation and the Surbiton Commissioners, but again the Bill was vetoed by Parliament. Undaunted, the Corporation prepared a third plan in 1899, but it was rejected after two days' deliberation by Parliament, who inexplicably declared it to be not sufficiently comprehensive.

This third disappointment came at a time when the London United Tramways Company were seeking powers to electrify their lines from Shepherds Bush to Hammersmith and Chiswick, and to promote new tramways as far as Hampton Court. The LUT therefore put forward a plan for Kingston, but the result was a heated controversy. The Corporation argued that if tramways were to be built in Kingston, they rather than an outside body, should do it. But a large section of townspeople felt it better to put the whole scheme under the private ownership of the LUT.

After prolonged dissension the LUT finally moved in with a service which was to establish Kingston as one of the major shopping centres of South East England.

Track-laying began in 1905 and was completed the following year. It was a gala occasion when, on 1 March 1906, the first electric tram entered Kingston over the Bridge from Hampton Wick. Three specially decorated trams set out to tour the new route attended by the Mayor, Councillor H. G. Minnitt, and the Managing Director of the LUT, Sir Clifton Robinson. However, the occasion was marred on Kingston Hill when a brewery dray-horse took fright and collided with the leading tram, hurling Sir Clifton into the road.

Kingston's first trams were beautiful vehicles with covered tops, but after only a year they were replaced by a cheaper, open-topped design which remained in use until tramcars were superseded by trolley-buses in 1931.

The trolley-bus service began on 15 June, the Mayor and other dignitaries touring the town in the first of the new vehicles. During their journey they passed the last tram, travelling back to its depot and marking the end of an era in public transport.

Trolley-buses continued in Kingston until 1962. Then they were taken off the roads to make way for the familiar red motor buses of today.

One of the most valuable local innovations during the last hundred years was the provision of a drainage system. As late as 1861 it was declared at a meeting of the Town Council that "there could not be a more disgraceful drainage in any town with a population of 16,000 than in Kingston". The town was compelled by the sanitary legislation of the time to disgorge all its sewage into the Thames, and both Alderman Gould and Mr. Merryweather have left eye-witness descriptions of dunghills in the streets, open ditches running alongside some of the most important thorough-fares, and the open sewer that ran down London Road, through what is now Clarence Street, to discharge a thick stream of raw sewage into the Thames. An equally foul open drain came down Kingston Hill, through Manningate Lane (now Park Road) to the Latchmere stream and thence to the river.

Many cottages were built on the banks of the Thames so their

sewage could flow straight into it, yet many families drew their
drinking and cooking water straight from this same river.

The *Surrey Comet* of October 1860 campaigned for better conditions
in Kingston's artisan homes:

> They possess no outlet whatever at the back, not even a
> window, so that the air cannot pass freely through them and the
> ceilings of the rooms are so low that a man of ordinary height
> cannot stand upright in them, [it declared].
>
> They are destitute of the most common necessaries for decency,
> one water closet being made to serve several dwellings. Some are
> without a sink of any kind, and the dirty water is brought out
> and emptied into the uneven gutters in the centre of the lane,
> and may be seen standing in fetid pools.

It was small wonder that epidemics were rife in Kingston. In
1838 more than one in twenty-eight of the town's population died
annually. By 1886, after the establishment of a proper sewage
system, the figure had dropped to less than one in fifty-nine. By
1904, after the enforcement of hygiene regulations and the appointment of a Medical Officer of Health, the Town Guide was
boasting that Kingston's death rate was only 13.6 per 1,000 of a
population of 37,741, compared with the national rate of 16.2.

The Kingston-on-Thames Improvement Act of 1855 had
enabled the Corporation to take long-overdue action by extending
the limits of the Borough and placing draining, cleansing, lighting,
paving and general improvements under Council control, and
authorising them to raise money for these purposes. A similar Act
of 1888 laid down health regulations, including the compulsory
notification of infectious diseases to the Medical Officer of Health,
and the authority of the Medical Officer to inspect farmhouses,
dairies, cowsheds and milkshops.

The building of a new, £16,000 underground drainage system
began in May 1864 and was completed in May 1865, though the
sanitary legislation of the time decreed that the ultimate outlet
must still be the Thames. However, the new sewers were so
shoddily constructed that within a short time they had become
almost useless. To add to the problem a Royal Commission
decided that part of London's drinking water should come from
the Thames so, in 1867, an Act was passed compelling all authorities above the Capital to divert their sewage from the river, and
imposing a fine of £100 a day on defaulters. This meant that

Kingston, and all the other towns concerned, were faced with the huge task of undoing all that they had legally been compelled to do.

Kingston managed to obtain a stay of execution but, as a glance at the *Surrey Comet* of the period will show, the question of sewage disposal became a nightmare to the town during the next ten years. The Corporation eventually solved the problem by an imaginative move. It entered into an agreement with the Native Guano Co. whereby, using a highly advanced chemical process, sewage could be divided into effluence fit to be discharged into the river, and sludge, which was dried, ground and sold at 3s. a hundredweight. The processing plant was set up in Down Hall Meadow, just north of the railway bridge, and operated until late in the 1940s, when the site was needed for a new electricity generating station.

The Corporation's Fertiliser Department issued a leaflet extolling the merits of "Native Guano", and delicately indicating its nature and purpose with a quote from Shakespeare's *Timon of Athens*: "The Earth's a thief that feeds and breeds by a composture stolen from general excrement."

Ultimately Kingston's Native Guano was being used by horticulturists throughout the country.

The town's sewage is now disposed of at a special works built near the Hogsmill River at Berrylands in 1957.

For centuries Kingston had relied on its Town Pump for a constant supply of clear spring water. It stood in the Market Place until the end of the nineteenth century and, together with many good wells in the area, kept the town reasonably supplied. But the rapid spread of Victorian Kingston, and the growing menace of pollution, made these sources inadequate and dangerous. However, no one yet realised the connection between dirty drinking water and disease—unclean air was thought to be the only reason for epidemics—so the sewage question excited far more interest than the activities of the waterworks companies who supplied London and its environs. There were eight operating by 1856, two of them situated in Kingston.

The Lambeth Waterworks Co. was established in 1785, and took its supplies from the Thames at what is now the site of the Royal Festival Hall. However, the river became so filthy that in 1852 the Company opened a pumping station, filter bed and intake system at Seething Wells. These were hot springs, a mile from Kingston's town centre on the Portsmouth Road, and believed for many years to offer a cure for eye ailments.

The Chelsea Waterworks was formed in 1723 at a time when the Thames at Chelsea was so pure that salmon flourished there. By the middle of the nineteenth century the river was so foul that, like the Lambeth Company, the Chelsea firm obtained an Act of Parliament to build a new plant adjoining the Lambeth one at Seething Wells. But periodic incursions of flood water from the River Mole caused both companies to open new intakes further up the river at West Molesey. The Lambeth Company's Molesey installation opened in 1872, and reservoirs were added in 1874 and 1903. The Chelsea Company began operating at Molesey in 1877, with an intake and four reservoirs. The water was then delivered to Seething Wells for filtering before being pumped to London.

The filtering processes used by both Companies began not for reasons of hygiene, but to make the water look more attractive. It was pioneered by the Chelsea Company, who were using the first successful slow sand filter bed in 1829. The relative immunity of the Companies' consumers in Kingston and elsewhere during the great cholera epidemic of 1866 proved the importance to health of pure water, and throughout the latter part of the nineteenth century Parliament imposed increasing controls over the water Companies. It also began a prolonged campaign to gather all the Companies under one control. Finally, in 1902, the Metropolitan Water Act was passed, and by 1904 all the Companies had been vested in the Metropolitan Water Board.

This legislation was of great benefit. Throughout the nineteenth century low-income families in Kingston had no water in their homes, but had to fetch it from the communal standpipe that stood in most of the squalid courts and alleys. The water supplied to these standpipes, and to individual houses, was only turned on for a few hours a day, so extra water was stored in open butts. Kingston's Horsefair—a huddle of Tudor streets and cottages—had such a butt, contaminated by dust, litter and animals, and shared by all the families in the neighbourhood.

A discovery that roused Kingston's dogged conservatism to white heat was that of gas. In 1833 John Bryant, a fitter from Maidstone, built a small gasworks in Kingston and piped a supply to a few houses. The townspeople were horrified, especially when the

Corporation unexpectedly sided with Bryant and his enterprise. A major reason for their hostility was the fact that Kingston candles had long been nationally famous for their quality. The town's candle factory, owned first by Ranyards and later by Smiths, had flourished since the eighteenth century, and gas was an obvious threat to this profitable industry.

A public meeting was called at the Guildhall on 25 July 1833, and a resolution passed "that the lighting of the Public Lamps of the town with gas will be a serious injury to all property situate within it, an inroad on the health and a fruitful source of discomfort, nuisance and litigation to its inhabitants, and will drive some away from the town to the injury of its owners and the increase of parochial rates".

A committee was set up to institute legal and Parliamentary proceedings. It included the Earl of Liverpool and other residents determined to prevent the "pipes and stenches" of a gasometer from coming into the town.

Undaunted, Bryant founded the Kingston Gas, Light and Coke Co. in 1835. But his little organisation had no exclusive powers or capital reserves, and a steadily increasing demand led to the incorporation of the Kingston Gas Company in 1854. As the demand for gas continued to grow, the Company obtained Acts of Parliament in 1859 and again in 1864 to increase its works and extend its powers.

The Kingston Gas Co. continued until 1930, when it was taken over by the Wandsworth, Wimbledon and Epsom Gas Co.

A major landmark in Kingston's history occurred in 1892 when the Corporation became one of the first municipal authorities in Britain to establish an electricity supply. A small power station containing diesel-driven generators was opened in Down Hall Meadow in 1893, and the town's first electric street lighting shone out on 4 November of the same year.

The plant was enlarged to keep up with the ever-increasing demand for electricity, but there were difficulties during World War I as all the plant machinery had come from the German firm of Siemens Brothers.

In 1945 the Corporation began building a gigantic new power station in Canbury Gardens, but the project was completed by the Central Electricity Board after the nationalisation of electricity in 1947. The new £6 million station was officially opened in October

1948 by King George VI, accompanied by Queen Elizabeth. During the ceremony the King was presented with a silver model of the new Hawker naval jet fighter to symbolise Kingston's long association with the aircraft industry. For one of the great twentieth-century developments of the town was the establishment of the famous Hawker Siddeley firm.

Its history began in 1912 when Sir Thomas Sopwith founded his Sopwith Aviation Company in a former skating rink near Kingston Station. He later acquired factory premises about 100 yards away in Canbury Park Road, but in 1920, after various vissicitudes, the Sopwith Company was replaced by the H. G. Hawker Engineering Co. with Sopwith and the brilliant young Harry Hawker on the board of directors. Only a year later Harry Hawker died at the controls of the Nieuport Goshawk he was testing for the forthcoming Aerial Derby, but his name has lived on in the firm ever since. In 1933 the Company became Hawker Aircraft and in 1935, after acquiring all the shares of the Armstrong-Siddeley Development Co., the Hawker Siddeley Aircraft Co. Ltd., was founded as a public holding company. The Company continued to occupy the Canbury factory until 1959, when it transferred all activities to its extensive premises in Richmond Road. One of the proudest boasts of the Kingston factory is that the famous Hurricane 'plane, used in the Battle of Britain, was first made there.

Other industries which have helped to shape twentieth-century Kingston are the manufacture of plastics, aircraft finishes, industrial paints and lacquers, cameras and precision photographic equipment, radar and microwave instruments and electrical transformers.

A fifth of Britain's wine production comes from a factory covering more than eight acres in Villiers Road, and believed to be one of the biggest centres of its kind in Europe.

Kingston is famous for many other trades and industries, and it intends to encourage others, for there are approximately 173 acres in the Royal Borough which are scheduled for industrial use by 1981.

Kingston is not given to looking back. If it did it would scarcely credit that not so long ago it was a backward country town, unwilling to contemplate any future beyond stage coaches and coal barges.

Sources

Much of the material for this book has been gathered from the primary sources referred to throughout the text. I have also drawn valuable information from the following printed works:

Chapter I

BIDEN, W. D., *The History and Antiquities of the Ancient and Royal Town of Kingston-upon-Thames.* 1852.

HOLINSHED, R., *Chronicles of England, Scotland and Ireland.* Ed 1807.

WHITELOCK, D., *English Historical Documents*, Vol. I, 500–1042. 1955.

CROSS, H., *The Kingston Coronation Stone and the Coronations at Kingston-upon-Thames.* 1956 (typescript in Kingston Borough Library Local History Collection).

WILKINSON, B., *The Coronation's History.* 1953.

JONES, W., *Crowns and Coronations.* 1902.

ROBERTS, A. J., *Anglo Saxon Charters.* 1956.

The Oxford History, The 13th Century. 1962.

The Oxford History, The 15th Century. 1961.

HYDE, EDWARD, EARL OF CLARENDON, *History of the Great Rebellion.* 1702.

MANNING AND BRAY, *History and Antiquities of the County of Surrey*, 3 Vols, 1804–9–14.

TATE, W. E., *The Parish Chest*, 3rd ed. 1962.

ROOTS, G., *The Charters of the Town of Kingston-upon-Thames.* 1797.

STOW, J., *Annales.* 1600.

LYSONS, D., *Environs of London.* 1792.

MALDEN, H., "The Civil War in Surrey, 1642", *Surrey Archaeological Collections*, Vol. 22.

KIRBY, *The Making of Early England.* 1967.

Chapter II

KINGSTON BOROUGH COUNCIL, *Guide to the Borough Archives*, 1971.

KINGSTON BOROUGH COUNCIL, *Official Guide to the Royal Borough of Kingston upon Thames.*
Victoria History of the County of Surrey, Vol. 3. 1911.
BIDEN, W. D., *The History and Antiquities of the Ancient and Royal Town of Kingston-upon-Thames.* 1853.
ROOTS, G., *The Charters of the Town of Kingston-upon-Thames.*

Chapter III

HILLIER, J., *Old Surrey Water Mills.* 1951.
KIRBY, D., *The Making of Early England.* 1967.
FINNY, DR. W. E. ST. L., *The Story of Kingston Bridge.* 1931: *The Tenterfield.* 1940 (Typescript in Borough Library Local History Collection).
CROSS, H., *Markets and Fairs of Kingston-upon-Thames.* 1956 (typescript in Borough Library Local History Collection).
Victoria History of the County of Surrey, Vol. II. 1905.
SURREY ARCHAEOLOGICAL SOCIETY, "Mediaeval Pottery in Kingston-upon-Thames", *Surrey Archaeological Collections, Vol. 45.*
BRAYLEY AND BRITTON, *History of Surrey*, Vol 2. 1850.
SURREY ARCHAEOLOGICAL SOCIETY, "Crop Returns for Surrey", *Surrey Archaeological Collections*, Vol. 64.

Chapter IV

MERRYWEATHER, F. S., *Half a Century of Kingston History.* 1887.
KIRBY, D., *The Making of Early England.*
FINNY, DR. W. E. ST. L., *The Royal Borough of Kingston-upon-Thames.* 1902.
SURREY RECORD SOCIETY, *Guide to Surrey Records.*
CROSS, H., *Mr. Treasurer, Kingston-upon-Thames.* 1955 (typescript in Borough Library Local History Collection).
TATE, W. E., *The Parish Chest*, 3rd ed. 1962.

Chapter V

CLAY, R. M., *The Mediaeval Hospitals of England.* 1909.
BROOME, H., *Kingston Union: the Beginning and the End.* 1930.
TATE, W. E., *The Parish Chest*, 3rd ed. 1962.

LELAND, *Itinerary in England and Wales in or about the years 1535–1543*, 2nd ed. 1744.

Chapter VI

FINNY, DR. W. E. ST. L., "Mediaeval Games and Gaderyngs at Kingston-upon-Thames", *Surrey Archaeological Collections*. Vol. 44.
LYSONS, D., *Environs of London*. 1792.
TATE, W. E., *The Parish Chest*, 3rd ed. 1962.
BRAYLEY AND BRITTON, *History of Surrey*, Vol. 2. 1850.

Chapter VII

MERRYWEATHER, F. S., *Half a Century of Kingston History*. 1887.
HEALES, A., *The Early History of the Church of Kingston-upon-Thames together with the History of the Free Chapel of St. Mary Magdalene, Kingston*. 1883.
KINGSTON GRAMMAR SCHOOL, Quatercentenary booklet. 1961.
SURREY RECORD OFFICE, *Kingston Schools*. Typescript. 1970.
Victoria History of the County of Surrey, Vol. 2. 1905.

Chapter VIII

FINNY, DR. W. E. ST. L., *The Church of the Saxon Coronations at Kingston-upon-Thames*. 1942.
MARTIN, J. T., *The Parish Church of All Saints, Kingston-upon-Thames*. 1969.
BESSE, *Sufferings of the Quakers*.
Dictionary of National Biography.
SAVAGE, J. H., *Non-Conformity in Kingston*.
HEALES, A., *The Early History of the Church of Kingston-upon-Thames*. 1883.
STURMEY, A. C., *A History of Kingston Congregational Church*. 1932.

Chapter IX

AYLIFFE, G. W., *Old Kingston: Recollections of an Octogenarian*. 1914.
CROSS, H., *The Old Town Hall or Market House* (typescript in Borough Library Local History Collection).
LELAND, *Itinerary in England and Wales in or about the years 1535–1543*, 2nd ed. 1744.

Biden, W. D., *The History and Antiquities of the Ancient and Royal Town of Kingston-upon-Thames.* 1852.
Puckle, E. S., *At the Sign of Ye Old Post House.* 1935.

Chapter X

Merryweather, F. S., *Half a Century of Kingston History.* 1887.
Metropolitan Water Board, *Fifty Year Review, 1903–1953.*
Wilson, G., *London United Tramways, 1894–1833.* 1971.
Kingston College of Technology, *Electric Tramways, Kingston and District.* 1966.
Seymour, J. B., *The Postage Stamps of Great Britain, 1840–1853.* 1950.
Robertson, B., *Sopwith—The Man and his Aircraft.* 1970.
Leeson, D. C., *A History of Kingston Power Station* (typescript in Borough Library Local History Collection).
White, H. P., *A Regional History of the Railways of Great Britain.*
Harper, C., *The Portsmouth Road*, revised ed. 1923; *London to Kingston—transport facilities by road, 1837* (typescript in Borough Library transcribed from *A new guide to stage coaches for* 1838 by F. Kelly).
Kingston Borough Council, *Official Guide to the Royal Borough of Kingston upon Thames.*
Bryan, W. C., *Bygone Memories of Kingston and Norbiton during the last half century, 1932.* (typescript in Borough Library Local History Collection).

Index

Postscript

In a book of this size, with a subject as ancient and interesting as Kingston, much has to be omitted.

World War II, for instance, when General Eisenhower, Supreme Commander of the Allied Forces in Europe, lived at Telegraph Cottage on Kingston Hill while planning the D-Day landings of 1944; the famous literary figures associated with Kingston, such as John Galsworthy, author of *The Forsyte Saga*, born at Parkfield, near Kingston Hill ... poet and novelist George Meredith, the ruins of whose mock gothic home still stand behind a filling station in London Road ... R. C. Sherriff, author of *Journeys End*, and Edward Gibbon, author of *Decline and Fall of the Roman Empire*, both pupils of Kingston Grammar School.

Eadweard Muybridge was born in Kingston and died here after a brilliant international career as a pioneer in cinematography. Florence Nightingale was a frequent visitor, Emperor Hirohito of Japan lived in Kenry House on Kingston Hill during his youth, while the Duke of Windsor often played at Coombe Hill Golf Club when he was Prince of Wales.

But Kingston's wealth of history far outstrips the space of any single book so these, and many other facets of its story, must, for the present, remain untold.